THE RELEVANCE OF THE FATHERS

The Relevance of the Church Fathers for Today: An Eastern Orthodox Perspective

Metropolitan Emilianos Timiadis

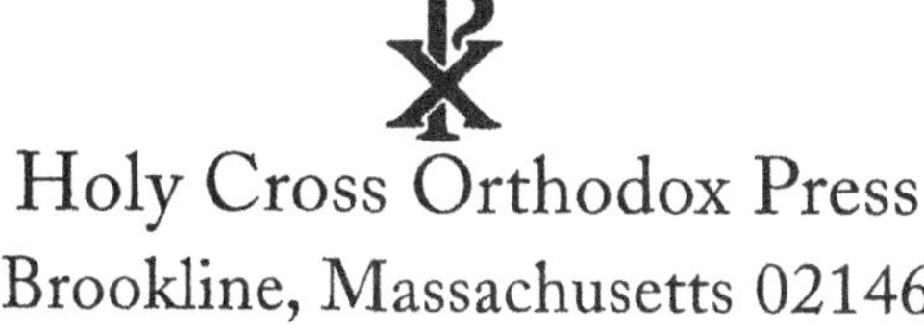

Holy Cross Orthodox Press
Brookline, Massachusetts 02146

Funds for the publication of this book
were graciously provided by
THE ARCHBISHOP IAKOVOS
Leadership 100 Endowment Fund

Published by Holy Cross Orthodox Press
50 Goddard Avenue
Brookline, MA 02146

ISBN: 1-885652-01-1

Contents

Introduction 1

Chapter One: Nothing Alien to Them 4

Chapter Two: The Authority of the Church Fathers 9

Chapter Three: Synchronic and Diachronic Wisdom 16

Chapter Four: Keepers of Memory and Continuity 22

Chapter Five: Ecology and Economy 28

Chapter Six: Profiting from All Positive Values 33

Chapter Seven: Suffering and Privation Are Instrumental in Life 38

Chapter Eight: The Fathers: Passionate Educators 46

Chapter Nine: The Only Sure Guides for Understanding the Bible 53

Chapter Ten: Tutors for Our Full Training and Growth 62

Chapter Eleven: Guides for Our Worship 68

Chapter Twelve: A Case Study 79

Chapter Thirteen: How to Treat the Heterodox 84

Conclusion 90

References 94

Introduction*

> Εἴ τις σκληρὸς τὴν ψυχὴν καὶ ἄπιστος ἢ καὶ φιλομαθὴς ὢν τύχοι, παρὰ τούτου—τοῦ 'Ωριγένους—μαθών, καὶ συνεῖναι καὶ πιστεύειν ἑλέσθαι ἀναγκάζοιτο τρόπον τινά, καὶ ἕπεσθαι Θεῷ λέγει ταῦτα οὐκ ἄλλως, οἶμαι, ἢ κοινωνίᾳ τοῦ θείου Πνεύματος. Τῆς γὰρ δυνάμεως δεῖ προφητεύουσί τε καὶ ἀκροωμένοις προφητῶν. Καὶ οὐκ ἂν ἀκούσαι προφήτου, ᾧ μὴ αὐτὸ τὸ Πνεῦμα τὸ προφητεῦσαν τὴν σύνεσιν τῶν αὐτοῦ λόγων ἐδωρήσατο.

> If anyone were either obstinate of soul and unbelieving, or anxious to learn, he might learn of this man's understanding and belief, and be forced in a manner to choose God and follow after him. And he declares these things, I think, none otherwise than by communion with God's Spirit; for the same power is requisite both to those who give utterance and to those who give ear to prophesies; one would not hear a prophet except the very Spirit which prophesied had bestowed upon him the understanding of its words.[1]

We have chosen as the introduction to the present study a remarkable sentence from St Gregory the Wonder-worker (213-270), a disciple of the great Alexandrian teacher Origen. Briefly, it summarizes the service which the Church Fathers rendered to humanity: to communicate the saving truths, to make them accessible and understandable in order that people may come nearer to God. This again implies a mutual sharing of the Holy Spirit, by the sheep and by the shepherd, as well as the speaker and the listener. Only on such a mutual basis can patristic wisdom be properly understood and communicated.

**A shorter version of this study was given as an address at ceremonies during which an Honorary Doctor of Divinity was bestowed upon the author by Holy Cross Greek Orthodox School of Theology, Brookline, Massachusetts in 1993.*

In this perspective, the Church Fathers can above all else be considered pastors of souls, guides, fathers in a much broader sense, interpreters and messengers of God's will. Man, in whatever state he may be, is in need of guidance and of counseling in order not to go astray. In an age of arrogant self-sufficiency and egoistic attitudes, rejecting any intervention from others, i.e., by parents, teachers or pastors, many may not see the salutary effect of those in a bygone age when the wisdom, the experience and the illumination of those saintly and inspired men and women were standing for the amelioration of society on the whole, and the Church in particular. When all provisions for a perilous situation became hopeless, only one word by a Father was salutary. Thus, the mouth of the pagan society seeing the courage of St Polycarp of Smyrna, exclaimed: "Behold, he is the doctor of Asia, the Father of Christians."[2] This expression means that, at the time of the composition of this text (second half of the second century) the title "Father" was in current use to designate a bishop, and it was not unusual for the pagans to attribute it to bishops.

Similarly, in 177, the martyrs of Lyons addressed the bishop of Rome in the following terms, "Father, *Pater* Eleutherios."[3] This name entails a certain authority, as conveying the conscience of the Church and being illuminated by God, interpreting all that concerns faith and daily life. St Basil of Caesarea added to the extent of such weighty views: "What we teach, is not the result of our own reflections, but what we have been taught from the holy Fathers."[4] This statement concerns his reference to the fathers of the Nicaean Ecumenical Council held in 325. Later St John Damascene collected a series of statements borrowed from patristic writings aimed at stating the orthodox doctrine on various important subjects.[5] In order to see the catholic dimension of this patristic authority, in the West, during the sixth century there appeared what is known as the Decree of Gelasius, *De libris recipiendis et non recipiendis*, offering the first catalogue of reliable Christian authors meriting consideration and those not.[6]

Thus from the very beginning we find within the Church and parallel to the place of the Bible a deeply rooted respect for pronouncements on ethics and/or doctrine by those saintly persons. The Church – and we use here the term in the most broad sense – was constantly referring to their opinions on this or that issue, holding that they express the truth. In many upheavals and confusing moments, with the opinions being divided, the extreme value of a convincing opinion echoing the conscience of the family of God was felt. Their personal experience constituted a solid basis and the most precious capital for discerning erring views from the true ones.

Chapter One

Nothing Alien to Them

It is surprising and a stumbling block for a non-Orthodox to encounter in Orthodox writings frequent references to what we call "the Fathers of the Church." Such frequency may give the impression that the Bible is undervalued or considered to be of less importance, or perhaps that patristics and the Bible have an equal authority. Such views are unacceptable, but how then can one explain such attachment to, and veneration of, the views of the Fathers, either of the East or of Latin Christianity? Do we Orthodox elevate their views to a level higher than the teaching of the Gospel?

The Fathers as a whole reflect the teaching of the undivided Church in general. They were not seen just as eminent theologians or highly qualified doctors of theology; they were also esteemed because of their depth, their unique spirituality, their life in prayer, their theological consistency, holiness and accuracy. A truth is conveyed or formulated not simply by the brain of an educated theologian, but also and even more so by a saintliness which is illuminated from above. Theology is not just another academic training or *gnosis*. It is the result of both knowledge and a life of prayer through which a man becomes reliable, charismatic, inspired and guided by the Holy Spirit. But not everyone can claim to be illuminated (cf. the abuses of the so-called "Charismatic Movement"). Genuine manifestations ought to be attested by the whole Church and confirmed and approved. Such approval prevents abuses and misinterpretations and tests the authenticity or pseudo-revelation of individual insight.

Patristics offer not only reason but also an inner intuition as the means of understanding the Bible. This key is often overlooked, this *synienai* of God's word contained in the words of man (Lk 24.45). The *synienai* of the Bible does not mean etymologically "to understand," but "to journey together with," or "to come together with," the Scriptures (Mt 13.14). In other words, the Bible will make sense only while travelling together with the insight, the hidden context and very meaning along their road. The Greek Fathers were always conscious of this key which opened the inner part of the Bible, so they could not be too concerned whether or not some passages were historical. They looked for the purpose contained in the Bible; they lined up with this thrust – the *synienai* (Mt 13.19).

According to St Basil of Caesarea, this view demanded clarity from within, that is, purity of the heart. The reason for this, was that the Gospel was the product of the early Christian community, which was a worshiping community permeated by *agape*, the selfless love of one to another, irrespective of ones own interests. This love as life, existence, is a dynamic expression of the fullness of realization, an impetus of innermost thirst. *Agape* was the disclosure of the purity of heart, and *agape* was the new commandment, because God is love (1 Jn 4.8). In using this key, it could be seen that all sacred books are interrelated. St Maximos the Confessor maintained that the Law is the flesh of spiritual man; the prophets are his senses. The *Evangelion* is the "noetic" soul, which works through the flesh of the Law and the senses of the prophets. Further, the Gospel really displays its power through the energies of the complete, spiritual man.

A Christian therefore examines the Bible to find a way of life, God's commandments, and he sets out to do what they say. He looks for the *synienai*, for that road to Emmaus which Kleopas walked when he and the other were joined by Jesus (Lk 24.13). While on this road, the Christian does not raise the question of what must be demythologized, nor does he expect one of the rocky mountains to jump up; he simply joins in when Kleopas says, "Did we not feel our hearts on fire as he talked with us on the road and opened throughout the scriptures to us?"

Assuming that our faith springs from Christ's teachings and that of his Apostles, then theology is its development and formulation by the most saintly people of God. We know that for the realization of the divine plan God has recourse to human cooperation. He chooses godly souls, entrusting them to put all their potential resources at the service of the saving *oikonomia* in the life of the Church. Throughout history the Fathers thus played a great role as regards the true interpretation of God's will and its understanding, and the further expansion of his kingdom. Such are our Holy Fathers – Cappadocian, Antiochian, Alexandrian, Syriac, and Byzantine. Hence, theology is patristic because it is based on the interpretation of the faith concerning how to comprehend the meaning of the revealed truth and how to apply it in concrete realities. They transmit the conscience of the Church from one generation to the other.

In addition, we hold patristic authority because in the most crucial times of distortion of the truth by heretics, the Fathers, with adamantine courage, refused any reduction, any bargaining, negotiation, or compromise. Thus, St Athanasios of Alexandria refutes the Arians' claim that they improved the Trinitarian dogma, stressing the importance of keeping the transmitted faith.[7]

The truth is undivided and it must be kept as such. The Fathers showed us the interaction between dogma and life, that every article of our faith is closely related to human reality. In fact, God used their mouths to preach the truth, diffusing it throughout the *oikumene*. If we turn back to those confused days when error was predominant, and orthodox views held only by a small minority, we can imagine what would have been the fate of true faith today without the struggles of the Fathers. Rightly then, St John Klimakos praises their task:

> He who has attained to stillness has penetrated to the very depth of the mysteries, but he would never have descended into the deep unless he had first seen and heard the noise of the waves and the evil spirits, and perhaps even been splashed by these waves. Paul confirms what we have said. If he had not been caught up into Paradise, as into stillness, he could never have heard the unspeakable words (2 Cor 12.4).
>
> The ear of the hesychast will receive from God marvelous words. That is why in the book of Job, that all-wise man said: 'Will not my ear receive marvelous things from him?' (Job 4.12)[8]

St Anthony the Great praises the virtues of saintly persons doing God's will in all things:

> Therefore God comes to dwell in them and gives them joy and sweetness, which feeds their souls, nourishes them and makes them grow.... When Ezekiel saw four living creatures, each with four faces, all showing the glory of the Lord, he was not in a city or a village but outside in a plain; For God said to him, 'Arise, and go forth into the plain, and there shall you be spoken to' (Ez 3.22). In general such visions and revelations were given to the saints only in mountains and wilderness.[9]

We have to remember that "theology" in the ascetic writings does not mean, as it does today, a systematic exposition of doctrines or theoretical knowledge relating to God. It means a gift of the Spirit, the gift of speaking about God with deep insight, with powerful words. It is given only to those who have also received the high gift of wisdom and have risen to that blessed state known as *hesychia*, contemplation; hence it is sometimes spoken of as if it were identical with these. St Isaak the Syrian is explicit on this subject:

> The Lord has reserved for himself men in the world who serve him and take concern for his children, and he has chosen for himself those who serve before him. For a difference in rank is not only to be seen in the affairs of earthly kings, where those who stand always before the king and are confidants in his secrets enjoy greater glory than those who are engaged in external matters. But the same can be seen in what pertains to the heavenly King: how much greater boldness is acquired by those who are unceasingly initiated into his mysteries by conversing with him in prayer, of how much more apparent is their mastership over all creation.[10]
>
> Hope awakens a natural longing in the soul and gives men this cup to drink, straightaway making them drunk. And they reckon things far off as near because all the parts of their soul are set aflame, as by fire, through their longing for what lies afar off.

> Thither, therefore, the whole content of their thoughts is directed, and they speed over onward to know when they will attain this. When they approach a virtue to practice it they do not practice it separately, but with all the virtues at once, completely and comprehensively. For they do not make their journey upon the royal highway as other men, but these giants select for themselves short-cuts, whereby gloriously they journey swiftly to the heavenly mansions. For this hope so inflames them, as with fire, that they cannot rest from their incessant and headlong course on account of their joy. There comes to pass in them what was spoken by the blessed prophet Jeremiah, 'I said, I shall not remember him nor speak his name. And there was in my heart, as it were, a flaming fire and it entered into my bones.' (Jer 20.9) Such is recollection of God in the hearts of men who are drunk who hope in his promises.
>
> I call the short-cuts (among the virtues) the all-embracing virtues, because they are not of great length as manifold pathways of a discipline leading from here to there; they do not await a time and place and they accept no distraction, but straightway they make their stand and accomplish all the virtues.[11]

Certainly, the extraordinary wisdom of the Fathers cannot be explained exclusively on the basis of their personal merits and gifts. They were, in addition, caught up by the Holy Spirit for whom they became heralds and instruments. St John Damascene recognizes this: "Through the Holy Spirit the Law, and the Prophets, and the Evangelists, and the Apostles, and the pastors and the teachers *(Didaskaloi)* have spoken."[12] It should be said here, that the Fathers were writing, living and acting within the mystery of the Church and never in an ecclesial autonomy of their own gifts. Speaking as children of the same Mother Church, and also as her teachers, they were building up the Body of Christ, the *Ekklesia* and striving for its growth.

Chapter Two

The Authority of the Church Fathers

We must, therefore, not only strengthen the inestimable services of the Church Fathers but also enlarge their contribution, in the wider sense, of building up the Church of Christ since Pentecost. This operation of constructing the body of Christ is twofold: depending largely on its very head, Jesus Christ, on the one hand, but also on his close collaborators, men and women, faithful to him. Such are the Fathers of all ages. We must never lose sight of the fact that Christ did not leave us a detailed written exposition of his will and how we should realize its execution. All the writings of the New Testament are rather accidental, occasional letters or instructions to individuals or newly established communities. In spite of such specific character, they include hints or implicit references to all-embracing truths, hidden and covered.

Thus, it was left to chosen, saintly souls to point out, to expose, to develop and dress these truths in the most appropriate terminology for the benefit of the people. This was their exceptional *diakonia* and as such it has an everlasting value. Let us remember the arguments of Arians against Christ's divinity adopted and formulated in credal form by the Nicaean Council of 325. They claimed that nowhere in the New Testament is the term found designating the divinity of the Son of God, equal to the Father and consubstantial – *homoousios*. A strong challenge to which St Athanasios of Alexandria gave the answer that in the Bible can be found *ennoiai*, meanings, and it was for later generations to uncover, formulate and interpret such important meanings.[13]

It is not without significance that later St Photios of Constantinople compares the Arians to iconoclasts and calls attention to the Arian claim that the word *homoousios* did not exist in Scripture, just as now the iconoclasts claim there is no scriptural support for the reverence of images.[14] In both cases, we have before us a parallel, namely that the arguments turn around the unwritten work. In the sixteenth century, the Reformers will repeat the same claim: that nowhere in the Bible does one find reference either to sacraments, to the Eucharist, to the authority of the Ecumenical Councils, or to tradition, communion of saints, episcopacy, etc. Their slogan *sola scriptura* explains all, namely only the written word, nothing else is acceptable. Photios' condemnation of Arianism is not due merely to his orthodox allegiance, but springs forth from a genuine incompatibility within him with its suppositions. To subscribe to Arius' dogma was to fall back into paganism, just as to accept iconoclasm was to deny a doctrinally supported and providentially ordained development in the history of the Church. Photios was filled with the vision of Christian progress down to the consummation of the doctrinal canon in his own day and beyond into the future. Along with many others, he was sure that the expansion and further growth of the body of Christ was entrusted to the wise care of God's co-builders who were unearthing hidden truths and giving to them the needed wording. Faith and theology were not static. They at the same time were containing, in an inclusive way, many other truths, in an embryonic stage, awaiting disclosure and development within the frame of Christian history. Behind the development of patristic theology we sense a vibrant, living Church of which the Fathers were the living embodiment. They rejected errors which appeared and reappeared because as historical phenomena they led nowhere and in their sterility ran counter to the very principle of their own being as instruments and mouths of the Holy Spirit.

This instrumentality is confirmed by St Gregory the Theologian (Nazianzos), applying to his own case the Psalmic verse: "In my desire for your commands I pant with open mouth and I drew the Spirit" (Ps 118.131). "I am the divine instrument, reasonable instrument, instrument to a good artist put into movement and adjusted by the Spirit. Yesterday the Spirit was dictating me silence. Today it knocks my spirit. I then shall sound the word and I shall contemplate my speech."[15]

In our days, much importance is attributed to the term "authority," rejecting anything else, which critically examined, does not correspond to the truth. In this context, the early saintly persons enjoyed uncontestable and unanimous respect, as incarnating the true evangelical spirit of the life in Christ. They were possessing what St Paul calls "Christ's mind" (Rom 11.34) and consequently being charismatic in the full sense, filled with the Holy Spirit. Such figures were accepted in the conscience of the worldwide Universal Church, as one can see from records by Rufinus, Palladios, John Cassian, St. Jerome, Socrates, Sozomen, Eusebios, etc. What has been said of St Anthony, equally applies to his biographer St Athanasios of Alexandria, who from the earliest was considered a Master of the spiritual life. This explains why St Athanasios qualifies his biographical treatise of *Vita Antonii* as "a full account of precepts on the life of a solitary in form of a narrative."[16] Precisely as such, St Anthony's biography rapidly reached the West and the rapid expansion of asceticism throughout Western Europe is due to this book. Modern theologians are unfair when they judge the East as overstating the importance of asceticism in those days. It suffices to remember that the great doctors of the Church had not yet distinguished between dogma, eucharistic liturgy, worship, morals, asceticism, or mysticism. They were treating the Christian religion as a whole, as indeed it is, one and simple. The *Encyclical Letters* of St Athanasios were very instructive in completing inquiries on thorny problems, and offering directives and right solutions. Thus, St Jerome highly esteemed such letters, recommending them for study to those thirsty for growth in spirituality. One example is that he advises the young novice Paula to acquire them and keep them in her library.[17]

It is a misconception that early the ascetics held narrow views. Indeed one finds quite the opposite, an astonishing openness, clemency and immense charity. The way leading to the summit of the life in Christ does not depend on wonder-working, healing, receiving visions or other gifts, but in being attached to God's will, attached to virtue. Such a life is not restricted to an elite few. The ascetic principles put down were not destined exclusively for a closed category of individuals, but for the general public. Although such admonitions were addressed to the disciples of the Fathers, at the same time crowds of lay people from all social classes were rushing in order to receive instructions: rich and poor, young people, soldiers, generals, high court magistrates, pagan philosophers and all kinds of intellectuals, sick people and those possessed by demons, deacons and priests and bishops, even the emperor and crown princes were often requesting advice by letter.[18]

All these were impressed not by a rigidity of the counseling, but by the flexibility, the gift of discernment. And it is amazing that everyone was taking the advice as if the words pronounced were destined exclusively for him.[19] People were mainly seeking spiritual guidance: how to face suffering, how to be liberated from temptations. For both St Anthony or St Makarios the task was to reach the suffering and needy soul, hungry for higher steps, longing for sanctification.[20] Their intention was not to seek candidates for the contemplative life, but to help and nurture every Christian.[21] In addition, monasticism as a religious form, was never absolutised as the unique way for salvation. The idea of perfection cannot be restrictive, applied exclusively to monks. A Christian within the world, can sometimes surpass the ascetic in his cell. Numerous stories have come to us reminding monks not to rely on being apart, or to sleep quietly in deceitful arrogance and security. Of course, the nature of such stories, naive and from rural life, were more understandable by people of poor culture, and the following is one of them:

> One day Anthony while praying heard a voice saying: 'Anthony, you have not yet reached the degree of sanctity of that of a tanner living in Alexandria!' To these words, the elder, early in the morning started the main road marching towards the city. Having found him, Anthony did not expect such reverence from the man, since he stood up moved by receiving such an illustrious visitor. But the elder said to him, 'Tell me what you are doing; because of you I have left the desert and come to see you here.'
>
> The tanner answered Anthony: 'Have I really done any good until now? This morning going out I was saying to myself: 'All inhabitants of this city, from the humblest to the greatest, will enter the kingdom of God, because they do right deeds; myself alone and my sins will lead me, I am afraid, to eternal punishment.' This is what morning and evening, before going to bed, I say to myself in all sincerity from my heart.'

> Then Anthony cried: 'Indeed, my son, by staying in the house as a good worker, you gained God's kingdom without being tired. While I have spent all my time throughout in solitude, and still I have not until now gained the degree of virtue manifested in your words!'[22]

This simple and little naive story shows that it is not this or that social state life which makes one a saint. There is only one sainthood: work, on the one hand, of the Spirit followed on the other, by man's efforts. If monks have chosen an unusual way, more sure perhaps, it would be disastrous to take pride in that. Perfection does not reside in the means being used. Many simple Christians may reach to a higher degree of perfection than many monks. It is not exterior practice which elevates, but interior solid and profound virtues.

The adjectives and most eloquent titles attributed to such godly men and women reveal their immense authority within the Christian family and even among pagans. They were seen as custodians of the faith, interpreters of the faith, conveying the very meaning of scriptural texts, physicians for spiritual healing, and guarantors of Christian discipleship. The words which the early (third century) *Apostolic Constitutions* recommends concerning the respect due to the bishops are not vain: "they are fathers after God."[23] St Anthony says, "Thanks to them, catechumens were baptized, been warmed by faith and been looked after as a hen does for the little."[24] Spiritual fatherhood was more than pastoral care and spiritual counseling by providing advice; it meant persons being entrusted by God to convey the right paths to be followed so that people may not stray into dubious deviations.

The rarity or total absence of such godly fathers in a given society was seen as a calamity deserving God's sorrow for human apostasy. In one instance it is recorded that brothers were frustrated by not finding such saintly guides and shepherds and started expressing their dismay:

> Some brothers who had seculars with them went to see Abba Felix and begged him to say a word to them. But the old man kept silent. After a long time he said to them, 'You wish to hear a word?' They said, 'Yes, Abba,' Then the old man said to them, 'There are no more words nowadays. When

> the brothers used to consult the old men and did what was said to them, God showed them how to speak. But now, since they ask without doing that which they hear, God has withdrawn the grace of the word from the old men and they do not find anything to say, because there are no longer any who will carry out their words.' Hearing this, the brothers groaned, saying, 'Pray for us, Abba.'[25]

Let us keep in mind that in this context, the term "word" – *logos,* for the Fathers of the desert, as in Pauline theology, has deep connotations. Through the "logos of the elders," people were able to communicate with the very source of wise instruction, that is God's Spirit.

Many centuries later, St Symeon the New Theologian (949-1022) more firmly developed the importance of such godly fathers used by God as instruments to communicate his will and to contribute as co-builders to the welfare of the ecclesial body, that is the Church. Because this divine-human body needed *synergoi*, competent agents, ministers, one sees in their persons the living presence of our Lord. Following his instructions the disciples consider and were firmly convinced as if they followed Christ and were with him. For St Symeon, a perfect father is the one being who changed and reached the icon of divinity, thus becoming the dwelling of the Holy Spirit and the focus of divine light from which all the others can put and borrow light for their souls.[26] Such a father is united with Christ, possessing the whole Christ within himself.[27] In this emotional text, St Symeon has his own spiritual father in mind, Symeon the Pious, abbot of the Studios Monastery in Constantinople.

Such spiritual growth, of course, is acquired through hardships, persistent humility, vigilant spiritual warfare and dominion over bodily passions. The more the material part of our fallen nature is subdued, the more the spirit grows and transforms the whole being. Thence the frequent dictum in ascetic language: "Give blood, and receive the Spirit." This expression comes from a saying of the Egyptian father Longinus: "Abba Longinus said to Abba Akakios: 'A woman knows she has conceived when she no longer loses any blood. So it is with the soul, it knows it has conceived the Holy Spirit when the passions stop coming out of it. But as long as one is held back by the passions, how can one dare to believe one is sinless? Give blood, therefore, and receive the Spirit."[28]

We are allowed to compare the perplexities and frustrations over the centuries to the children of Israel who, led by Moses out of Egypt, wondered, "Where are we going?" and "When will we get there?" The Fathers were encouraging Christians to live with questions for a while without fearing that everything would fall apart. At the right time these remarkable persons offered the needed answers. Thus, they have made an enduring contribution to the development of what is known as the patristic spirit, an ever present source of living wisdom.

Patristics is more than a precious heritage. The Orthodox family has been shaped by its resources, yet the Church Fathers' spirit and authority has grown bigger, nurturing many other bodies. They inhabit a household built to endure stress. From outside, the winds of an ever changing world blow. Inside the family, the ebb and flow of argument simultaneously threaten to shake the foundations, or to halt new achievements. The Fathers, confident in Christ's lordship over his Church, reconcile new ideas and confirm old views. Whether it is the past or the future, foundations or final capstone, the Church in her ongoing mission feels the security that comes from a tradition and the freedom to think anew.

Chapter Three

Synchronic and Diachronic Wisdom

If we consider and propound the Church Fathers' message as everlasting and relevant to every time and every place, it is because man's problems remain fundamentally the same: weak, inconsistent, impotent, though he claims to be almighty he is sometimes unmerciful to others and self-indulgent about his own faults, prone more to evil than to good, trusting more his own resources than God's mercy, leaning more upon the earth than upon the unperishable things of heaven. Although many socio-political conditions have changed, and many ideological revolutions have tried to improve human life, yet he remains with an unsatisfied heart, waiting for something else, known and yet unknown at the same time.

Christian ethics and the consequent pastoral therapy from time to time require changes, adaptations and a more efficient approach to human wounds, as they encounter the continuing tragedy and misery of the human condition and destination. This remark leads us to another consideration. Although patristic wisdom is eternally contemporary, transhistorical and diachronic, when it comes to action, we must draw out the best, the essential, the relevant, avoiding any uncritical and hasty application. It is therefore folly to make literal use of patristic texts without a scrupulous examination of the morphological, contextual, and cultural changes which have intervened in history. Authors who simply present in their writings numerous quotations, one after the other, forget two factors. First, that it is not enough to enumerate references in order to convince the reader. Second, the real art is to extract the essence, avoiding secondary items, emphasizing only what is relevant and applicable for their times.

Human beings suffer, and will continue to do so in order to reach the most perfect state of happiness during this earthly pilgrimage. Their grave mistake, often, is that this pursuit is done only periodically, advancing now but after setbacks, or without perseverance, or that it is done arbitrarily using only a small number of virtues. There is no place for such selective ethics. Some use such a method in vain. They adopt a few virtues pleasing to them, rejecting the rest as unbearable or unattainable. Such an attitude produces discredited half-Christians, who easily betray the fragile, incoherent edifice. The Fathers, however, teach us wholeness, integrity, inner harmony and unity.

Man should always seek to discipline his base passions, be trustful in God, vigilant about his self as always in revolt, and struggle for the promotion of his inner world. The road is filled with thorns and temptations, but equally available is succor from God and his Church. The distinctive Christian effort makes man different from the animal world: always refusing to yield, always resisting, always placing fences and protective barriers against the violent attacks of passions and instincts. If he does not give order to the chaos around him, then he loses the very goal of his life, his destination. This would result in a continuous life of vulnerability, of returning to his primitive state of losing the necessary equilibrium. The great issue of today, raised by our generation – "Why live?" – "What is the purpose of life?" – is not just a present issue. It has always preoccupied humanity. The Fathers dealt with such vital existential, anthropological and metaphysical inquiries with profound care, led by God's Spirit.

In dealing with them, the Fathers were aware of the trap of dualism, of treating the body and the soul as if they were two entities, autonomous, and impossible to co-exist. Evangelic spirituality or Christian *askesis* is nothing more than the overcoming of the inherited fallen nature by continuous exercises, always being sustained by God. Such a promotion results in the subduing of our will, cultivating self-denial. Determined to follow a most ordered effort, the desert monastics did not torture or mortify the flesh, as some source of evil, but showed what its place is in the Christian realm and in the order of creation. By following such an itinerary, one can find the true meaning of life, a foretaste of eternity, St Isaak the Syrian says: "Nobody can reach the heavenly kingdom by learning, but rather by continuous *askesis*."[29]

Because human life is fluid and changeable like the waters of a river, the Fathers use a variety of language and arguments. Even if their language seems to us bitter, severe or even uncharitable, one fact remains: they really love the world. They see with penetrating eyes an earthly existence full of contradictions. One effort seems to fight against another, so that true Christians in their eyes, become a selective minority. They see man destroying what he has raised up. The whole of life seems full of imperfections and illogical acts. But life's outlook here is different from what it is in heaven.

And yet, in the midst of such misery and contradiction, they do not resign themselves to becoming pessimists or misanthropes. St Gregory the Theologian describes man as "designed by God from the very beginning,"[30] marching towards his fulfillment. With Christ's incarnation the door for union with God is opened, the way to *koinonia*, the divine sonship.[31] The Logos becomes man, in order that man can become divinised in him and the children of Adam will be promoted to becoming sons of God, as St Athanasios of Alexandria states.[32]

The Fathers are aware of human decline and ugliness but instead of turning their eyes away in disgust, they exalt God's philanthropy. Thus, St Methodios of Olympos exclaims, "What greater thing exists than having a God who is a friend of mankind with a philanthropic incarnation?"[33]

One may ask: Are they not blind, not taking into account also the darkest aspects of human rebellion and sinfulness? It is true that the Fathers did not speak on this point more than what was necessary. Contrary to St Augustine's obsessional dilemma regarding original sin, for the Fathers, sin did not constitute the integral part of man's nature. It was, rather, a later unnatural intruder having no real hypostasis as St John Damascene states.[34] They pass by such an unnecessary problematic as St Maximos the Confessor explains: "The previous teachers of the Church, avoiding to say more on this matter preferred to be silent, considering it more profitable not to go deeper. This reluctance was due to the fact that among many believers it was impossible to seize the very depth of all that was written on such an important subject."[35]

In the above statement, one clearly sees the recognition of our human limitations in penetrating many aspects of dogma, and consequently the reasons for recourse to apophatic theology, so dear to St Maximos and many others. While they encouraged critical theological research, at certain moments (realizing human incomprehensiveness) they stood only in awe and respect. Finding a refuge in apophaticism is supported by the ancient Plato, who stated that true theology can be rendered only "in poems, tragedies and verses."[36] Aristotle also stated that the first originators of theological concepts were Homer and Hesiod. It also suffices to have a look at the liturgical hymnology of the Orthodox Church, where we find that most of the articles of our faith are, in fact, in texts of doxology, an insight shared by St Gregory the Theologian, St Symeon the New Theologian and others.

It would be wrong to regard these Fathers as idealistic moralists, proposing a millennial ordered society, in terms of utopian futurology. Knowing that the world around them was desperately seeking a better life, by indicating the uniqueness of the Gospel, they spoke about the uniqueness of Christ, as Savior and Redeemer. To transfuse hope, a theological hope, they described the liturgical feasts as realizations of God's promises.

There is a colossal gap, of course, between theory and practice. Nobody denies it. Though the Church was proclaiming this hope, the daily picture was most unfortunate: anguish, despair, sadness and discouragement were, and still are today, depressing symptoms. The daily press speaks of morosity, sad moods, nervous stress, but above anything else, souls are empty. If a great number of souls are dead, the Fathers did not hesitate to point out that they are dead to the hope – *elpis*, because mainly they are dead to the sanctifying grace. Evil, in whatever form, diminishes our aptitude to God's grace. The Fathers, with boldness, declare that a society with its members is submerged, inundated by an ocean of sins, the gravest of which is a contempt for and the forgetting of our creator, our God. Whatever sector we touch, political, economic, cultural, intellectual, we seem nearer to the time of the ancient Roman decline than to any loyalty to God's will.

Today much of the publicity about unemployment risks diverting our attention from its real causes. Perhaps the most felt and visible of the social dramas is begging. But this and many other manifestations are only consequences. Economic recession is not a blind irresistible flood where men are innocent victims. We speak of corruption, scandals, insecurity, criminality, fear – the list is long. What prevents us from proceeding to a true diagnosis is the apathy and resignation of many. They lack sensitivity, unable to react in order to take initiatives, to get out of this terrible impasse, only caring for "bread and spectacles" as in the Roman Empire.

The Church Fathers insist that God's plan has not changed. Equally, too, the real problem of human tragedy is not found in sociological upheavals and injustices, so much as above them and beyond them. Often a tree hides the forest. The worst damage done by a desacralised era is to turn attention elsewhere, which results in moral laxity, religious skepticism, spiritual despair, with further declining signs, paralyzing any healthy effort for renewal and recovery.

Patristic hope is that of a Savior, working *spes contra spem*, hope against every other hope (Rom 4.18). This is so because Christians become men and women of the impossible. That is, that what is seen with secular eyes as impossible, becomes possible, Christ working within us and with us. Without him, even the most economically or technologically advanced societies become a devastated desert, where only amoralism, materialistic civilization of the *hic et nunc,* pure nihilism grow.

Evangelical life does not invalidate a given culture for a society. It brings it into communion with an inculturation process, injecting its properties, the light of our God of love, incarnate in Jesus. This metamorphosis takes place in the Church, a place *Locus ubi Deus quaeritur,* a place where God is sought. And this God is not, as in the ancient pagan world, idle, withdrawn, and indifferent. On one hand, the Old Testament prophets do not cease to proclaim that "our God is a living, acting, intervening, God, not like the dead idols." On the other hand, Plutarch, a contemporary of Christ, echoed the perplexed ancient philosophers, writing: "The waves around the island of Paphos murmured: God, the Pan died, a new God is being born." The patristic synopsis of this incarnation was resumed by St Athanasios and taken later by St Augustine, namely, that "God became man so that man may become God." In this promise and conviction lies our joy, our confidence for this thorny life. No one, therefore, can remain idle, inactive, neutral.

Everyone is challenged to reconsider the "why's" of his existence, even when the majority does not bother to know, refusing even to spend time for such reflection.

If we firmly advocate the close relevance of patristic thought for today, this does not mean that we should renounce ethics today. Rather we should realize that such ethics is partial, selective, rational, hedonistic and individualistic. It is based on utterly wrong aims to improve well-being, to encourage satisfaction of our desires in the short term and to reduce, as far as possible, our sufferings. These motivate all concerning life and social justice. We are in a plain biological reductionism. Thence the efforts and embarrassment on genetic issues concerning prenatal diagnosis. From what point of conformation can one justify abortion? Do we simply seek to avoid hereditary sickness or rather to modify genetic patrimony? How can one live knowing that in his fifties he is going to develop Alzheimer's disease? We forget that this world and the life we live were given to us as gifts by God, and hence are in need of the highest respect. Even if man can do all, he must not do all.

The Church Fathers understand Christian ethics as a unique aid to help in finding a meaning to life, an orientation, and a way. From this point of view, it is positive, beyond abstract interdictions of morality. It helps us live another style of daily life which respects others, as well as the natural environment. If animals and plants can exist without us, the contrary is not true. We are part of the interdependent earthly community. In order to eat, to live, and to grow, we must turn to nature. It is not right in the name of man's superiority to mistreat nature. Man is a fallen being, and, by experience, we all know how easily one becomes selfish, violent, unreasonable and abuses his rights. Modern society is so complex and vulnerable and the possibilities of destruction so great, that a single monstrous act can cause enormous damage to humanity.

We must take care so that technology not be allowed to go too far for example by absolutizing nuclear power on the pretext of producing more energy. Thanks to God, there are still fantastic unexploited energy resources. We are not deriving enough energy, for instance, either from the wind or from the heat of the sun. We must also be more inventive in revising our methods of production and our understanding of work and of time.

Chapter Four

Keepers of Memory and Continuity

Every human being is bestowed with an extraordinary faculty, namely memory, the ability to remember the past, his own and/or events around him. There are things to be remembered forever, if not he loses his orientation in life, falling, collapsing. When God delivered the Decalogue to Moses and to Israel, he outlined the primary duty of man to *remember* the true God, Yahweh, against the polytheism which surrounded the Israelites. This was also the task of all the prophets, in reminding the people continuously of the divine commandments, of the true worship against idolatry of the Assyrians and Egyptians. The pious Psalmist states that "the wicked have laid a trap for me, but *I do not forget* your law" (Ps 118.61); and again, "I am unimportant and despised, but I do not *neglect* your teachings" (Ps 118.141). The whole of Psalm 118 is a public confession that the godly man must always have in mind the will of God, which is the only deterrent against transgressing God's will and going astray.

This continuous memory of God by man reflects the degree of attachment and love of his soul to his Creator. Whoever loves continuously remembers the person of his love. The ascetic teachers will develop this as a cardinal virtue, God's memory. St Basil of Caesarea comments: "This is dwelling in God, to solidly establishing within us the memory of God. Only thus do we become 'the temple of God.' "[37] St Gregory the Theologian develops this virtue at length:

> It is much preferable to remember God than to breathe. One does not exaggerate if he says that above anything else

> this should be done, as it was already been said by Moses: 'Remember these commands and cherish them. Tie them on your arms and wear them on your foreheads as a reminder. Teach them to your children. Talk about them when you are at home and when you are away, when you are resting and when you are working. Write them on the doorposts of your houses and on your gates...' (Deut 11.18-22).[38]

Nilos the Ascetic (380), offers a practical directive, that "as we breathe the air, in the same way we must unceasingly praise and worship the Lord, even if we are surrounded by earthly worries. A wise and disciplined spirit is able to continuously remember his creator."[39]

In this connection, we must remember that Church history is not intended to offer to the coming generations merely records of events and places, but rather to keep in a living memory all the saving acts of God's love in his community of believers. Heretics, upheavals, dark forces, dissensions and so many other adversities did not succeed in stemming the advance and growth of the Church's mission in the world. When Eusebios of Caesarea recorded the historic adventures of early Christians, providing a catalogue of the opponents of the Orthodox faith, he did this work in order to enable Christians to remember the intervention of God and his continuous presence in the struggle of Christians and the survival of his church. Theodoret of Kyros (395) is the author of histories both of the Church[40] and the *Philotheos Historia* or *Ascetica Civitate,* [41] avoiding any scientific or secular motivation. From the very beginning of this treatise, he points out: "All that the preceding generation of spiritual athletes achieved either in the desert by fighting demons, or the martyrs by accepting death for the sake of Christ's love, the main target is the same: to show to future generations the sufferings of so many saintly individuals so that they may draw lessons and might follow their example. Thus, continuity will be assured."[42]

The worst state of an alienated soul is to be cut off from this communion of saints, by avoiding any remembrance of such past events, by ceasing to remember God's presence and his dependence, by establishing a wall around his self-sufficient attitude. Thus, he becomes a total amnesiac, suffering from amnesia, which means isolation, self-imprisonment, ingratitude and contempt towards God his benefactor. It is this phenomenon that the Fathers had to face by becoming "reminders," directing and healing our memory. In doing this, they refer to martyrs, to the sufferings of generations of true believers. One thing they try to keep alive is the fact that nobody can live by himself, in not sharing and rejecting the achievements of all past soldiers of our common faith.

This memory is dysfunctional in these days. So many attractive elements of our technological era obscure the past, drawing our thoughts towards futile things. Such deviation destroys spiritual health. Isolation, decay and gradual degradation, bring us to the stage of refusing to turn to God, to our true self. Thus our memory is distanced, irrelevant to our main duty to care for our soul.

Strangely enough, many others are passionate about things of the past, thinking they could heal the turmoil of today. They think of the past in terms of a magic remedy effective enough to exterminate our uncertainties, our doubts and anxieties. Thus, the past appears as a savior and introduces a sort of continuity to a present exposed to all kinds of aggressive events, abrupt changes, gods of versalities of the daily life. The Fathers also refer to the past but in quite different terms, and for them the past fortifies us in our fight against forgetfulness, against collective amnesia, characteristic of frequently manipulated public opinion. Further, the past again restores to its glory the grandeur of our famous ancestors.

It has become a passionate hobby to turn to what is old, to history, archeology, archives, and monuments. Even the United Nations has asked all countries to venerate what is declared as a national antiquarian patrimony. Parallel to all this, festivities, anniversaries of past events are filling our calendar. We are reminded that modern man must not forget the past. There are many syndromes for returning to the past, to tradition, while other forces press us to obliterate those same traditions.

In these days, commemorative celebrations are multiplying, because man must not forget the past. The past is offered in small parcels of anniversaries. This commemorative hysteria becomes an integral part of our culture; in some way keeping alive our own identity. One sociologist described our age as "the age of anniversaries."[43] The sad side of it all, however, is the unwillingness to draw lessons and examples from past events. The role of the Church Fathers in constantly referring to the past, *paradosis* – tradition, is quite different. Being guardians of the past, they at the same time live their values in order to show their everlasting significance, their relevance for every time and every place. They incarnate this past as "priests of commemoration," filling the gap produced by the loss of authority and of stable reference in a given society. Tradition – *paradosis* thus becomes a dynamic past, a living and inspiring force.

Such a dynamic view of the past, which is not passive and sterile, becomes for the Fathers a must against the danger of loneliness in history as uprooted erring beings, secularism, when lay movements try to replace the religious cycles and liturgical rhythms of life, by exalting sociopolitical instead of religious heros. Thus, in civil history, we see how in the recent past strident nationalism has succeeded in establishing as a civil religion events of temporal nature, offering a different interpretation of our existence. Thus, anthropocentric humanism is strengthened and great men and women become the alternative saints of the Church. In such cases, with temporal models absolutizing them while undervaluing the intemporal saints, we see the futility of such commemorations. They seem like footprints in the sands of time which surely will be washed out with the next tide.

The Gospel says that a wise man "takes new and old things out of his storage room" (Mt 13.52). In the same way the Fathers although not belonging to their time were not its slaves; they were adapting the old and making it new – *nova et vetera.* A Christian must love his time; it is an imperative evangelic truth. This does not mean he approves of the decline, the vices and evils current of his day. Loving my time where I live, means willing its good. It is not to be thrown to the frenetic moral chaos of the time. Loving my time means to want the moral progress of the men of my time, by accepting and properly using all authentic progress, art, science and technique. It means, also, remaining free from the slavery of the fashion of ruptitude, both immobilism and rupture. The Fathers while reminding us of the past, were revealing the renewing power of the Holy Spirit to a total new vision. They know how to communicate the old as new, as current for today, actualizing in the present the plan of God. Here one can remember the task of the Eucharist which re-actualizes an event which took place two thousand years ago, and in celebrating it one feels as if the Cross and the Resurrection take place just now, before our very eyes.

Until recently disproportionate attention was given to research and theological study. Many scholars sought to scrutinize and to clarify the history, evolution and development of dogmas, with emphasis on critical text, philologic and grammar. Another history, very close to this history of dogma, which we could easily call history of dogma embodied in and applied to the life of Christians, is now drawing more and more interest. From such studies emerge the main characteristics of godly persons and their impact on the moral standards in a given society, on Christian personhood as quite distinct from non-Christians. Such study inevitably touches the whole realm of ascetic spirituality in the first centuries and its tremendous influence on ethical behavior in parishes in our time.

We know that asceticism, or monastic ideals and values, existed even in the days of our Lord but in an embryonic state. Asceticism and monasticism are two ideals with reciprocal interpenetration. Asceticism, as the nucleus of evangelical ethics, prepared the way for those who had a passion for higher moral standards to flee the world and to live the main values of Christian perfection either as a solitary or in a community. *Askesis*, such as is described briefly in the New Testament, is the spiritual doctrine proposed for those souls earnestly seeking perfection. It is outside the scope of this paper to raise here the varieties, morphological and exterior forms of different ascetic tendencies. They vary according to local traditions, but mainly influenced by the leaders and charismatic people who greatly influenced their disciples and consequently, created a sort of ascetic distinctive spirituality.

The core of such research on true evangelical spirituality, however, is made difficult because of the historical distance in time. How do we catch sufficiently their technique and knowledge? Are surviving texts complete and trustworthy? In those days, it must not be forgotten, the doctrine of Christian perfection was mainly taught orally, and much more by the living example than by words. If by chance, a master was treating in written form spiritual questions, this did not aim for us to interpret it as an ascetic rigid system of that bygone day. Being composed in view of a practical lesson and in order to meet the needs of particular persons in particular circumstances, the fragments we possess today, are not sufficient to recreate a complete schema. Further, the information from such texts came to us through indirect information of a few disciples or by tradition. How, then, in the light of such poor traces is it possible to reconstruct a faithful picture of the amazing life of those Christians?

In spite of so many disadvantages and inevitable gaps, it becomes, however, possible to reconstruct the general traits of early spirituality. Thus, the extraordinary spirituality of the first Egyptian ascetics did not invent new original directives, but only continued in a normal process of previous period and prepared that for the next following period. Different pages, certainly, but belonging to the same book in different times. We must bear in mind, that nobody in the early period claimed the title of teacher of spirituality, except perhaps St Clement of Alexandria. All those who were responsible for pastoral nurture did not pretend to substantially invent new things. They simply continue, developing and perfecting what was acquired in the first centuries. In the technical sense of the term, the true Master of the perfect life must be considered St Anthony the Great, who trained a great number of disciples.[44]

St Anthony was drawing and aspiring in the rich tradition and air of the Church of Alexandria, created by St Clement and Origen, disciples of the school of Pantainos. These did not exist in handbooks, but only in the example and the teachings of the leader. Thus, "the Lord granted Anthony for the benefit of others, in order that in the ascetic life from all that he had learned himself from the Scripture, many disciples may have him as master."[45]

Chapter Five

Ecology and Economy

It is not at all strange that the Fathers were very sensitive to nature and ecology, matters which today are of crucial importance. Specialists in environmental and ecological problems are not exaggerating when they affirm that abuses against nature are threatening the very survival of humanity. In his treatises, we find that St Basil of Caesarea continuously refers to the immense utility of nature and makes useful observations on animal and vegetable life. These offer edifying lessons for human beings, he says. What they have as imminent, man has to do by his own free will. What is implanted in animals by nature must be accomplished by humans through reflection and reason, and with authority. He even recommends that we study nature's behavior, looking into its evolution in the forests, in the countryside, as a kind of open school accessible to all.[46]

In fact, nature in our technological and industrial era is alienated from human respect and partnership. The natural world risks destruction due to a paroxysm of more and more production. This is because of man's wrongful approach to natural resources and his alienation from them, thinking that he can endlessly exploit all their potentialities. We forget, for example, that a tree is our friend. And yet this robust, proud big tree is at the point of dying, not due to any natural cause, but because of our ill treatment and destructive attitude. This forest is condemned prematurely, before its time. Its loss may one day plunge us into despair; in acid rain and ozone destruction, we see human selfishness and a brutal attitude. Man has completely forgotten that even plants possess a certain sensibility and can react. Ancients knew the mysteries of nature better than our present materialistic civilization. We consider nature in terms of continuous consumption and our own selfish, limitless profit and pleasure. Why do we forget that nature is destined for quite another purpose; that it is not simply a reserve of raw materials? We have become so concerned about our selfish comfort, that we do not even know how to communicate with our fellowmen and our natural environment. It is not astonishing that we have long since ceased to hear the voice of alarm which nature is uttering.

Occasionally, we confess that if trees suffer because of our pollution, our physical health will also feel the effect. We know that if the forests disappear one day, this will provoke many catastrophes. Biologists inform us that if plants are sick, the replenishment of oxygen in the atmosphere will suffer badly. And yet, our natural environment does not, in fact, demand extreme sacrifices. What the Earth does is to put before us a primordial choice. We have to choose whether to continue our present style of life or opt for a real change. If we choose the first alternative, sooner or later we will move towards an ecological catastrophe. If we choose the second, the vicious circle in which we are caught will be broken, and a renaissance of our natural world will become possible. But to achieve this, it is necessary to change our state of consciousness. It is time, after all, that as creatures we become once again integral parts of nature, of the Earth and of the universe.

In our world, no part is superior to any other. Each part is in solidarity with all the other parts and is interdependent. When a forest in Brazil is destroyed, our life is also directly effected. When an animal species disappears, all the animal world suffers its effects, and so do we. When an earthquake occurs in Japan, Europe feels the repercussions. When a volcano erupts in some corner of the earth, the consequence to our own environment is perilous.

This is why man must rediscover his rightful place in this universe. Turning from his selfish view regarding production and economics, he must adopt a respectful attitude toward the creation of God in giving rather than in receiving. Only then will there be an equilibrium, a harmony replacing his present hostility toward nature and its resources. Indeed, trees are and remain our friends. Consequently, we should love them. It is time to be reconciled with ourselves and with nature, this wonderful gift of the Creator.

Until the last century this beautiful nature was scorned and disdained with such expressions as *nature mort* – something dead, without soul and worthless. But the Fathers describe nature as the most beautiful ornament of the Creator. It is enough to read the relevant homilies of St Basil of Ceasarea on the *Hexaemeron*, while St Gregory the Theologian sees God as the best artist and designer: "The Logos artist has joined everything together. It is a real ornament – Cosmos as has been said, with an incomparable beauty. Nothing since has been conceived more bright or more magnificent."[47]

Athenagoras the Apologist sees the whole of nature as a chain of unparalleled beauty, and because of this, it is subject to admiration and is impossible to replace: "Its beauty is not made by itself but by a hand, that of the Creator, and with a plan elaborated by God."[48] This writing, sent to Marcus Aurelius and his son, Commodus, about A.D. 177 and here the philosopher shows to his readers the origin of the world relating it to the unique God of the Christians. Because of such a generosity of the Creator the inhabitants within his creation should behave decently and treat it properly. Therefore, ecology is followed by economy both terms applying to the nature of our habitation from birth to death, but also to management, use and/or misuse.

The term *oikonomia* is often used by the Fathers for God's attributes in ruling, taking care, and governing. Methodios of Olympos in Lycia, writing against the dualism and determinism of the Valentinian gnosticism writes: "A divine *oikonomia* exists and is the power of a supreme degree which rules all, which it is right to name as God."[49]

Noteworthy is that St Gregory, in order to describe the operational actions by Christ, uses the verb "uniting"[50] like a churchly body by which he means being gathered together, the assembly of all, the earthly and human, as well as all together in the Creation, even those gone astray, those erring, convoking all to oneness. He then deals with such a united assembly.

Over and against such a divine project stands man's resistance and arrogance, violating and ignoring limitations and God's sovereignty over the cosmos. He forgets that he is a mandated administrator, an *oikonomos*, an appointed steward, bound to use creation properly not surpassing the Creator's established boundaries in exercising his entrusted commission. The present ecological crisis with the related human degradation has its roots in the alienating march of a selfish, anthropocentric civilization. Every day there are so many atrocious crimes committed against nature. Man, never the absolute master of this universe, must be reminded of his limitations, subordinating his selfish projects to a more general imperative, remembering that this universe belongs to all inhabitants, present and future, and that every violation effects the participatory partnership of others living on other continents.

Fasting, therefore, is not only some isolated privation imposed upon our body, but a real sign implying a wider privation in many other areas of natural resources. One's avidity will indirectly have repercussions on nature as well. Individual self-satisfaction is an unnatural view of happiness, a disrespect for the communal character of humanity and a refusal to see that many other generations, now and in the future, have the right to share God's blessings as well as ourselves.

Man in various ways comes into contact with nature. He influences it and is influenced by it. His attitude, his treatment of natural resources, determines the present situation and even nature's future. Consequently, by respecting himself, by restricting his insatiable appetites, he succeeds in keeping the bio-earthly system in balance without serious disturbances. Practicing asceticism for the environment in this respect is valuable beyond any estimation.

The actual disruption of ecology and its catastrophic consequences are caused by the fact that technological man has not understood that scientific progress and fantastic achievements in the spatial world could not only be a good friend, a useful benefactor, but also a tyrant, a potential enemy, threatening not only his spiritual health but also the natural milieu in which he and his children must spend their lives. More and more industrial output for a more and more consuming society cannot really lead to true happiness unless some limits are imposed.

Voices are raised from many quarters for an ascetic culture, a disciplined mode of life, slogans which centuries ago were launched by the Church Fathers. St Gregory of Nyssa refers to such an approach with his vision of a world where the *microcosm* and the *megalocosm*, that is, man and the whole natural cosmos, come to an agreed, just cooperation, reconciled into one harmonious entity, with a close relationship, mutually sustainable, where the supreme rule will be order, a coherent march, as in musical harmonization, all these reflecting the harmony and unity of the first archetype, that is, the Creator and Ruler of all.

This coherent coordination and trustworthy cooperation between all constitutive elements, creatures, both creation and Creator, will prevent any diversion, anomaly, dark forces and subservient undermining. God's victory then will be manifested through all in a glorious movement – and only virtue – *arete*, will prevail.[51]

Thus, we understand how the relationship of man to nature should be: not as the absolute ruler or irresponsible dictator, but as *oikonomos*, as steward for its proper use and enjoyment. This is the meaning of the two verbs we meet in the creation story of the Book of Genesis (2.16): working and guarding. In the patristic mind both these economies, namely one by God to his creation and the other by his image – man – to the same creation, are inseparable. This close cooperation is a pact signed when God placed Adam and Eve in Paradise. Man must avoid any misuse, forgetting his limited assignment. He is not an absolute and everlasting owner giving account to no one. He is accountable. If he violates this principle, then he will reap thorns and suffering, as we are doing today. The possibility of destruction and ill treatment is the nightmare of an alienated society when it thinks that the material world is insensible and not living. We do not take the trouble to look upon the daily consequences of abuses and hostile treatment of nature's resources.

Man is destined to be the *leitourgos* of nature, offering as he does in the Eucharist the material elements of bread and wine to God and acknowledging both to come from him: "Thine own, of Thine own, we offer to Thee, for everyone and everything."[52] And man's place in the universe cannot be that of a high-handed selfish individual, arrogant; he is not permitted to profane, but rather to sanctify, respecting the integrity of man's creation. Leontios of Cyprus (sixth cent.) shows the context of such a worshipful diakonia by man: "Myself with the heaven, earth, sea, wood, stones, relics, temples, the Cross, angels, and men, with all the visible and invisible creation, to the Creator of all and Master and Maker alone, I render respect and veneration and worship."

Chapter Six

Profiting from All Positive Values

Contrary to the narrow approach of ancient philosophy by Tertullian, that "there is no relation whatever between Jerusalem and Athens,"[53] the Church Fathers deeply appreciated constructive elements and teachings of the non-Christian ancient world Between heaven and earth there are many common points, so that a spirit-bound disciple cannot ignore or exclude all that came to us from the pre-Christian world.

Not only in our days but even earlier times, human beings experienced two distinct sentiments about the true life in Christ: fascination and dislike. The first, because one admires and respects those who succeed in overcoming low desires and earthly passions and ascend to a higher moral level. The second, abhorrence, because its moral demands disturb those weak in the flesh, asking them to overcome bad habits, ways of life to which we have been tied. It has never been easy to drive away and escape from deeply rooted evils. The Church Fathers knew human nature quite well. And they never ceased to repeat that true man is the person who overcomes fallen man in his weakness. As long as he remains human, in the fallen state, he is not true man; he is just a child of Adam, badly in need of passing to another state by mastering his passions, desires, all the negative heritage of corruption and vanity.

A simple reading of their cultural milieu reveals to what extent, then and now, the prevailing culture was anti-ascetic, eudemonistic and permissive. It was and is based on a wrong assumption of allowing all human capacities to be freed, and every desire, need and appetite to be satisfied. From this point of view, patristic ethics reflects the Gospel wherein "violence against self," renunciation, crucifying one's self, abandonment of the old man, reduction of earthly need, portray the hardships and the unceasing spiritual warfare. Instead of attachment to worldly attractions, what is required is detachment – *apotaxis*; instead of a consuming and voracious life, reduction and austerity. The true finality of man is not achieved by encouraging possession of more and more, but a discernment of what contributes to his true development and growth. Thus, even the world economy should be based upon ascetic principles, in order to help solve the whole issue of environment and the disorderly use of natural resources.

One of the Church Fathers' targets was to fight an easy and hasty identification of happiness with prosperity. Instead, they introduced another principle, strange for many, that "one should give one's blood in order to gain in return one's spirit," meaning that fighting and warfare precede virtue.[54] Equally, that eagerness for solitude, stillness, curbing one's appetite were the only guarantee for true liberty. It is a revolutionary thought that the axes of true life were not pleasure and *hedone* nor material well being. What counts is the quality of liberty, to be truly free, to be liberated from one's self.

Today there exists a paroxysm of emphasis on endless rights and complete liberty for self-satisfaction, as being the only factor in the development of personhood. This idea animates, unfortunately, the whole spectrum of education and modern pedagogy. But this was not so even in Greek classical times, which was frequently praised by the Church Fathers for its ethical stand. When they developed evangelical ethics, they were aware even more systematically of the deep significance of two prevailing key terms: *agoge* and *morphosis*. Both were seen to complement each other, one as cause and the other as consequence.

The word *agoge* etymologically derives from the verb *ago*, which means to guide, to lead. It infers the whole realm of instruction. Since *agoge* leads to a process of learning, it implies that the quantity of knowledge is not meant to stay idle, as sterile capital, but should open perspectives for further shaping character, to form a superior being where knowledge, properly guided, serves for the building up of appropriate human behavior. In the field of education, the word *agoge* originally meant the leading of a child to the school by an adult *pedagogos*, but later it came to mean the whole process of responsibility for education. This is why, from the narrow field of primary schooling, it became used in order to refer to a wider effort, the lifting up of human weakness to higher horizons. We find such an application of the term in Plato dealing with paideia: "Paideia it is true, is the drawing of children and education towards certain principles of behavior which the Law designates as right and which also most of the pious and oldest, owing to their experience, accept as right."[55]

From this passage we notice that Plato understands education as an active process – *energeia*, seeking to create in the soul of a child *holken*, that is attractiveness, interest, cultivating a deep attention so that he might be acquainted with the principles of true human conduct, seen as the only right by the state, acknowledging it as the only true way. Here, continuous education is seen as the bringing up of an immature child, realized through the, of the developing soul's impulse towards the right rule of human life. Aischylos the poet uses the term paideia as the art of promoting the uncultivated soul toward a perfect one. In his tragedy *Seven on Thebes*, through Heterokles, he calls the mother "the most dear feeder and nurse, who from early childhood nourished citizens, undertaking and assuming all the accompanying labor for their education."[56]

Human nature is assumed to be lazy, resisting its amelioration and promotion, therefore in and need of a forcing effort, hard discipline and self-restrictive measures, so that the inner forces may find a favorable setting for expansion against the animal and natural instincts. This essential element for human realization of one's true self, obviously demands austerity and privations, imposed either by the self or by all those responsible for true well being: educators, parents, and religious instructors. Athens in those days was the world's workshop for high training and uplifting process through the most perfect pedagogical methods.

Why was such moral significance attributed to paideia in those days? Because most of the philosophers knew well that material food and mere knowledge do not change man's inner world. Human nature should be cleansed from harmful and undermining elements. It should be freed from darkness, disorientation and the disfunctioning of the mental forces of will and thought, to be elevated to the light, where it escapes from shadows and deceitful phenomena, and enjoys the essence of being. It becomes clear that such an educational effort cannot be restricted to children alone but extends to all people until the end of their existence. It is in such a context that the saying of Solon, the wise Athenian could be understood: "I become older, but always I am being taught." Edifying and improving our being becomes a continuous process which concerns every aspect of life till the last moment of our earthly existence.

The ancient world was conscious of the distinct value of body and soul. The body is subject to dissolution, degradation, decomposition, while the soul is immortal, eternal, beyond any human value, a truth expressed so clearly as supreme value and axiology by Plato: "Because in the same being coexist soul and body, nature dictates and recommends strongly that the one be dominated and subjugated, while the other – the soul – rule and be sovereign."[57] Further, Lucian points out that such physical exercise as gymnastics, does not seek exclusively the good state by the building up of the body, but produces much wider effects for the benefit of the *polis*.[58]

Such a reasonable and balanced judgement, becomes relevant today when, body-building has produced the trap of a new idolatry of the body, when sports are only played for the sake of sports alone or even worse, for the sake of the gambling of money. The spirit and ideal of the Olympic Games as originally conceived by Kentauros from Pelion, consisted in cultivating physical exercise to be sure, but equally to promote noble competition, as a duty to God. Such games were interrelated with courses in arts and spiritual exercises. Only thus could humans attain what is *kalon k'agathon*, that low instincts be dominated and creativity be developed. A higher and higher idealism was nourished so that one never stays idle and petrified. Education was a harmony, a movement of all faculties towards higher goals. The slogan did mean a utilitarian, profit making effort but a much higher endeavor.

The Church Fathers with their openness, deeply appreciating them as a reflection of the eternal Logos, made all these positive spiritual values of the ancient world their own, incorporating them Christian ethics, as preparatory steps. St Gregory the Theologian contested Julian the Apostate who said Greek culture was alien to the Gospel. Julian's identification of Greek philosophy with paganism alone and claiming that Christians could draw no useful material from such philosophy was refuted by St Gregory. Culture and wisdom belong to all, according to Gregory, and they are inspired from above. Christians, therefore, can profit from all that is healthy and constructive. Gregory answers Julian: "You pretend to use Attic language and culture? We, too, are Attics, drawing from the same sources whenever we feel necessary."[59]

St Basil of Caesarea wrote a monumental treatise concerning its value, showing the close connection and the valuable contribution of the ancient world: *Admonitions to Young Men on the Profitable Use of Pagan Literature*. With masterly eloquence, he recommends strongly to students to use as much they can for sharpening their intellect, to use classical literature so that they might grasp the deeper sense of Holy Scripture. They must imitate the bees which seek only the honey and avoid the poison. The pagans, too, bear witness to goodness and give palms to virtue.[60]

Such a reconciliatory and positive attitude towards non-Christian ethics and ideologies has an encouraging bearing on all values and cultures which Christians encounter today. We live in a pluralistic society. Christians traveling come across many sects, many beliefs coming from other continents and instead of choking us they must be seen as signs of God's presence, however imperfect and partial they may seem to be. Without rejecting them at once, or coming to an open conflict, it is better to look on the good side of them, their complementarity to what Christianity offers without, of course, falling to the other extreme of syncretism or relativism. Before the coming of the patristic wisdom, St Paul preaching in the Aeropagos of Athens reassures Athenians, Epicureans and Stoics alike as being very religious (Acts 17.22-23). The Christian writers referred to this harmonization, thus elaborating a most perfect synthesis of Hellenism and Christianity.

Chapter Seven

Suffering and Privation Are Instrumental in Life

The current massive effort to diminish or completely eliminate pain from daily life shows how unrealistic we are and how we miss the inestimable services it renders. Patristics reminds us that the time of trial and testing may also become a time of ascension and perfection. The early Christian writer, Tertullian (ca. 197), addressing the provincial governor of the Roman Empire, observed that "the blood of the martyrs is the seed of the Church" – *semen est sanguis christianorum.*[61]

Why should this be? Part of the answer is obvious: the love and bravery of the martyrs convinces us that their faith is real and in their lives we catch sight of the power of the crucified and risen Christ at work. But there is surely more to it than that. In addition to showing courageous faith, the martyrs also remind us of an aspect of every baptized Christian's vocation: to follow and to shape one's own life according to the model before us: Jesus Christ. They testify to a Christ who died a painful and humiliating death. Ever since the conversion of the emperor Constantine the Great, Christians have been in danger of forgetting this aspect of their faith. In past centuries, and even in our own time, in certain quarters, Christ has been used to legitimize earthly pleasures and potentates. His community of believers has been comfortable and assured, unwilling to disturb the peace and to speak a prophetic word, hesitant to take a stand against the stream of the world. But because of the sufferings and tears of the few, we can be optimistic about the Church. They teach us that ordinary, faithful life is never wasted; that ultimately the only adequate response to the evil we see around us is a life well led.

In dealing with such a vital subject, we must bear in mind the uplifting and pedagogic nature of sufferings. Our human nature is fallen, degraded, unhealthy and consequently badly in need of frequent interventions for its restoration. St John Chrysostom underlines another aspect: that the suffering and wrestling Christian reveals God hidden and working in him and through him. Those outsiders watching, unable to explain the secret of such endurance and serenity, soon discover that God's Spirit covers, sustains, protects and enables the sufferer to maintain his high spirit:

> Many of them were previously trembling, fearful, but after the reception of the Spirit, they were brought before wild beasts, fire and many other tribulations. They started to speak with such courage, that their listeners were astonished. Because the Spirit had remade them from clay to become as steel, rather flying like birds on the high, so that they do not fall down like other humans. Such is the power of the divine grace; Nobody, therefore, should excuse himself, as being with a body, he cannot attain a supreme state, and be unable to acquire virtues.[62]

St Gregory of Nyssa points out another aspect of suffering's role: to prevent us from blind submission and enslavement to worldly pleasures. Realizing to what extent deception, disappointment and emptiness arrive in this world through pain, we are awakened in time and warned to turn elsewhere:

> None of those things usually done in daily life, as pleasures, can fill our deepest needs, but as the Book of Proverbs tells us in an enigmatic way, 'every dealing with pleasures is like a jar with a hole on the bottom' (Prov 23.27). By bringing water frequently to such a jar, they discover at the end that they always remain unfilled and that their efforts are fruitless; because such people, while they pour continuously up to the bottom of their desire, trying to enjoy more and more sensual enjoyments, these people in fact never reach a satiety of the desire.[63]

As earthly pleasure is deceitful and misleading, one needs a constant reminder to avoid its pitfalls and to turn towards the direction of true joy, filling thus our jars with irrefutable happiness. If Christians turn in this direction, pushing away worldly attractions, such an unusual option is not due to lunatic fanatism. They are not despising this world, the marvelous creation, with a Manichean disdain. They firmly believe that truth and the genuine quality of our existence is found elsewhere. St Maximos the Confessor made a thorough analysis of this:

> A virtue gets its true becoming when the soul willingly and in a responsible way gets away from the flesh. Our soul is filled with spiritual joy when it disciplines the inherent troubles of the flesh. It is very natural, that after that the senses become impotent, and the soul turns rather towards virtue, the senses thrown away and marginalized and inevitably then the senses will be in pain...The senses will be deprived of operational mobility and the forces which manipulate the soul, unable to intervene.[64]

In seeking happiness, man often follows false objectives. He must refrain from such vain pursuits. We are made for another target, beyond corruptible goods, since in the deepest of our being there exists an immortal and everlasting hunger waiting to be satisfed. Such existential investigation did not escape the attention of the Fathers. They state that nobody can remain neutral while on earth, reserving and postponing his allegiance to somebody other than to his Creator or to the principalities of darkness, the Evil One. Nobody can remain undecided for a long time, hesitant, on the threshold; he must sooner or later make a decision. His inner world is waiting to host, to receive one or the other guest. In striking lines, St Irenaios helps us to see the effects of an indecisive attitude, harmful from many points of view:

> Do know that every man is either empty or completely filled. If he does not possess the Holy Spirit, then he does not know his Creator. If he does not live according to the Logos, to the celestial law, then he is misbehaving, living unjustly. Such a person is empty. But if he has advanced to God who has said, 'I will make my home with my people and live among them; I will be their God' (2 Cor 6.16; Lev 26.12; Ez 37.27), then he is no longer empty but completely filled.[65]

If for the economists, well-being is judged by an ever increasing income, more properties and more and more earthly goods, this is in stark contrast to the evangelic outlook where what counts is that which contributes to our inner development. Industrial output became a key to success and progress. The whole of our civilization is based on a poor spiritual effort, the emphasis being placed upon eudemonistic and anti-ascetic conditions. The whole nucleus of modern economics is anti-ascetic, encouraging unlimited spending of money, more and more consumption, all in order to make the factories work. Such an approach, ignoring the spiritual nature of man is devastating, it leaves man without spiritual resources and therefore unable to face adversities, illness, death, and so many of the tragic conditions which are inevitable in life. From various definitions given in our days, one can give credit to one in particular: that the worth and value of a human being is as "a possessing being" and not as " a being possessing reason." In other words, the true measure, the eternal values are sacrificed upon the altar of possessing and sensual wants. Avidity animates education and many motivations among migrants, how to get more and more. Urbanism, concentration in impersonal cities in a disorderly way, resulting in housing crises, pollution, little contact with nature and anonymity, etc. "To have" or "to be?" become two vital, challenging questions for modern life.

Such materialism does not lead to the fulfillment of life, but to its failure. Such a way of life takes from us too much and offers us very little in return. It takes everything, above all that which we have as our most precious possession, our soul, and in return gives us back futile satisfactions and a terrible, sad vacuum. It makes us slaves to ourselves, since it fuels all our passions, unsatisfed desires and endless worries. St John Chrysostom recommends us to keep away from such a confused situation, those worries and frustrations, by pointing us in the proper direction:

> We are not superior by increasing our needs, and we are not inferior because our needs are little....Nothing makes us so much slaves as when we have many needs. Also, nothing makes us free as to have only one need....This is why Christ, wanting to make his disciples superior to the others, being sent to preach to the whole world, liberates them from all these worries. He gave them wings, a way of life more rigid

than steel. Nothing fortifies the soul, as to discharge one from such obstacles; and nothing else weakens it more, if such things are not released.[66]

It is a terrible situation with such a degraded life when man is no longer free, but a slave multiplying day by day his needs, beseiged by all media channels to buy new things, to continually rush for new models. This avidity for more and more can be stopped and circumscribed only by imposing an ascetic approach and guide. *Askesis* means limitation. If there is none, then liberty has gone, and with it independence; in reality man is the worst slave of all kinds of publicized goods, often unnecessary and harmful for human personhood, integrity, and moral security. The result of such distortion is the abysmal inner emptiness in modern society, resulting in neurotic disorders.

Once such futilities become absolute in life, man begins to consider them most dear and indispensable. And if one of them is missing, then he suffers all kinds of psychoneurotic disturbances. It is a fatal blow if we dissociate the element of self-sacrifice and renunciation from our life, by claiming that one cannot live without, let us say, smoking, or watching long films on television. These needs then take the place of other values, chasing God from the center and instead placing there earthly things. This is another kind of self-worship, or as the hymnographer St Andrew of Crete says in his Canon read during Lent: "one becomes *autoeidolon*" that is a self idol. So many evils spring from an anti-ascetic mode of existence. Few unfortunately, were able to understand the deeper implications of *askesis* relevant to human destiny and right direction. Dispelling any narrow view, as if it concerns only withdrawn, solitary monks, *askesis* is a way of a balanced life, and one which makes it meaningful.

The damage is greater when we consider that such permissive misconceptions are detected even among modern theologians, who see theology not as ascetic and liturgical, but when they defend complete liberty and a compromise with all forms of vice and man's excessive needs. And yet, austerity is not an alien factor in Christianity; it constitutes an undivided, inseparable element of the Gospel. Nobody has the right to eliminate or belittle self-denial, the cross from Christ's teaching. The utility of such a restrictive pattern of life must not be forgotten. Not only does it help us spiritually, but the body is healthier and the mind clearer. St John Chrysostom refers to such benefits:

> Keep away from luxury and stay close to the modest life. What gains has the rich person who engages a multitude of servants, butlers, waiters, and cooks, who seeks the most rare of wines, paying high prices in order to satisfy his desires? Such a person falls down, lower than a slave, becoming the worst of slaves. No real pleasure is found in his life, but rather he pains and worries day and night; thinking on all his numerous staff. While one who lives ascetically is a slave of nobody. He is master of all. In all security he enjoys the light of the sun, is insensible to bad weather, and he is not afraid of difficulties. Anger does not excite him or hate, jealousy and other worries; his face is not wrinkled. His soul is calm like a peaceful harbor with quiet waters where storms cannot enter. He pursues his way with serenity, a very quiet march leading him to heaven, without being trapped by earthly goods which try to deviate his attention elsewhere.[67]

The Fathers see in the true restrictive life of Christians not only a distinctive model, but also the very incarnation of Christ's kenotic teaching. Such a life is many sided and profitable not only while on earth, but also because it is the pre-requisite for the life after death. Thanks to such lives, humanity has achieved much and men of brilliance have taken amazing initiatives for socioeconomic ameliorations. True artists, authors and thinkers are experienced, in different degrees, in asceticism. True humanism cannot be other than this when joined to a self-denying life, restricting fleshly appetites to the minimum. It is in this perspective that the analyst must see a Christian's orientation against tide, time, even against history. He wants to write a new history where the spirit is master over both flesh, earth, selfishness and ugly passions. A redeemed Christian must be distinct not only from animals, but also from other fellowmen who behave like animals.

Keep in mind that the true life in Christ involves an endeavor on the part of each of us to come nearer to God so that we may become one with him. We should not be surprised that such an effort can be found among many ancient thinkers who were quite overworldly for their time. After all, philosophy has always been a striking search for truthfulness. Such eternal dialogue with truth has animated generous spirits to deny their own self in order to reach as much truth as was possible for the pre-Christian era. Imposition of such restrictions was advocated by the Socratic philosopher Antisthenes, who said "I would prefer to become mad rather than to fall into pleasures,"[68] because hedonism meant a loss of inner liberty and the dispersion of mental faculties, preventing study and serious contemplation. The same Antisthenes took pity on those who were extoling the supremacy of luxury, sensuality and enjoyments: "I should wish that into such sensual satisfactions only my enemies' children might fall and not myself."[69]

Antisthenes' pupil Diogenes, an eccentric Cynic thinker, established as the principle of life an "inner liberty." To him nothing important in life can be obtained without ascetic restrictions; with asceticism everything can then be overcome.[70] All those ancient philosophers who spoke of self denial had a certain degree of affinity with Christians, seeking perfection by stressing inner liberty. If an ascetic willingly chooses the desert or the isolated monastic cell, equally a pre-Christian man practices austerity, rejecting earthly possessions and living instead within a large jar, like Diogenes the Cynic philosopher. Thus, the Stoic Epiktetos was saying: "Free is he who lives as he wants." One is deeply impressed by the Fathers openness towards the positive classical pre-Christian values. Most of them, having studied in pagan schools and academies, knew from their experience the immense intellectual resources found in them, another sign of God's Spirit spread throughout the pre-Christian world. This attitude is known as the presence of the *spermatikos Logos.*

Even further, for the ancient Greeks education was not a simple contact with a given civilization, nor with some local intellectual wealth. It went much deeper and further towards an ethical influence whereby acquired *gnosis* would be properly used and orientated to an ethical *telos,* or finality. True learning is found when a human being is elevated, transformed in his interiority and in cultivating high quality feelings, in other words, it implies a religious background as a solid reference and animating force. Plato expressed this fundamental principle in the statement, "Every science or knowledge if separated from virtue is degraded to evil and is no longer true wisdom."[71]

The appearance of errors and heresies, however harmful as they may seem to be, were instrumental in stimulating the convocation of councils. Christians throughout the ages were not anathematizing tribulations and sufferings. In times of strife and violent persecutions, they came together more often, for consolation but also for mutual strengthening, convoking regional synods and more general councils. Their size depended on the regional needs and real conditions. What is noteworthy is the positive attitude and dynamics seen in the suffering for the expansion of faith.

St John Chrysostom in assessing adversities, invites reconsideration of their usefulness and immense creativity if properly used:

> What then if he be evil, you say? So much the greater is the reward. Even for his wickedness you ought to feel grateful to him; even should he be evil after receiving ten thousand kindnesses. For if he were not exceedingly evil, your reward would not have been exceedingly increased; so that the reason for not loving him, the saying that he is evil, is the very reason for loving him. Take away the contestant and you take away the opportunity for the crowns.
>
> See you not the athletes, how they exercise when they have filled the bags with sand? But there is no need for you to practice this. Life is full of things that exercise you and make you strong. See you not the trees too, the more they are shaken by the winds, so much the more they do become stronger and firmer? We then, if we be long-suffering shall also become strong. For it is said, 'a man who is long-suffering abounds in wisdom, but he that is of a little soul is strongly foolish' (Prov 14.29).[72]

Chapter Eight

The Fathers: Passionate Educators

Assuming that the Christ-centered life is an unceasing process throughout one's earthly existence, the patristic approach to life may not seem too joyful. In secular terms, especially in our days, life must be enjoyable without restrictions and interdictions from above or from outside. But against such a defeatist conception, comes an encouraging assurance, that the Christian struggle is taking place within the context of God's sight, his affectionate care and infinite philanthropy. He is with the fighters, intervening and supporting them and the only thing he wants is that his followers' struggles go on, even aside from relying exclusively on God's protection and mercy. The whole family of God – clergy, monks and lay people – must be found in the ranks of soldiers, denying their selfish passions and sinful will, their self-reliance, and instead of these wearing a new armor: humility. "It is not visible signs and privations which will determine our salvation, such as fasting, vigils and sleeping on the ground," but "because I became humble, the Lord saved me" (Ps 114.6), St John Klimakos reminds us.[73]

Such an austere control does not imply disfigurement of human personhood, or self-punishment leading to inner conflicts and neurotic anomalies. Rather, it is a strong antidote to a disobedient and continuously revolting will. It is a counter-revolution against the human revolution transgressing the divine will. It is precisely for this reason that uncompromising spirituality has no signs of sadness, despair and melancholy. Joyful fighters! A gloomy Christian fighter is by no means a Christian one. Because such endeavors engender joy and liberation, restore of distorted beings and fill one with hope and joy, just as a person suffering in the hospital and waiting for surgery, anticipates already the happy outcome and the return of his health, being full of anticipated joy.

How then to refute the allegations that patristics are obscure, anachronistic, enemies of legitimate joy, fanatically forbidding a good life in terms of secular criteria? But ascetic soteriology does not rely so much on ascetic disciplines and penitential manifestations: fasting, almsgiving, weeping or renouncing this or that. Rather, it is based on an inner relationship, a Christian being related to God in his inner heart and not only by his exterior deeds. In the *Sayings of the Fathers* it is said that Abbot Pambo made it clear: if you keep your heart upright, then you can be saved. It is in the depths of our being, in the heart, that the great struggle between good and evil is played out, the struggle between our allegiance to God or to the Devil. A life, even the most religious one, practicing all the rules of asceticism, if it does brings feelings of God within, is most monotonous, dissatisfied, complaining, capricious and peculiarly unpleasant to others. Such superficial religiosity can easily be detected. Inversely, true *askesis* never leads to isolation, loneliness, rejection of the world or exclusive concentration upon attainment of one's own salvation, ignoring all others. True life in Christ, on the contrary, unites us with God and our brothers and sisters. Salvation, after all, is not an individual activity. We cannot march towards God and at the same time turn our back on our fellowman.

Of course, in working towards human solidarity, Christians must find a balanced attitude, so that horizontal duty is not at the expense of the vertical, or vice versa. The more one reaches God's *koinonia*, the more one becomes charitable to his brothers and sisters. And the more one is alienated from God, the more one becomes egocentric and anthropocentric. The measure and criterion is not selfishly to be always looking within, but a consciousness of being sinful which can be an instrument and a channel for God's love. Rightly, Abba Mathoes observes: "The more one reaches God the more one sees himself a sinner."[74] Such an elevated soul, consumed by divine eros, is guided in all things by supreme love. As St John Klimakos states, his comment referring to the value of chastity kept mainly thanks to a supernatural denial of what one is by nature, "so that a mortal and corruptible body is competing in a truly marvelous way with incorporal spirits. A chaste person is someone who has driven out bodily love by means of divine love, who has used heavenly fire to quench the fires of the flesh."[75]

If we push our inquiry concerning the authority of patristic sayings further, we discover that in the Christian conscience and even much earlier in the Old Testament belief, only saintly persons merited the right to give admonitions and to interpret the ultimate truth, the secrets of God. They possessed not only astonishing human wisdom and knowledge, but even more, a personal piety, a true gift of the few beloved by God. Their uniqueness lies in their experience of complicated daily realities, as St Isaak the Syrian says. He advises people in despair to seek counsel not from highly educated men, but from people with deep experience, who by intuition know what is going to be profitable in the course of events, and what could be damaging. Many things which at first sight seem to be profitable may with deeper insight be just the contrary. To such persons we should run for instructions. Not everybody is trustworthy to give advice, except the one who has mastered his freedom and fears, not the accusations and slanders against him.[76]

We thus see that the whole ministry of patristic counseling and the exposition of the dimensions of our faith is the outcome, not only of the Fathers' acquaintance with the Bible, but above all, of their personal faith and piety of their being continuously in communion with the Holy Trinity, and consequently, guided and inspired. For every visitor approaching them, it was easy to sense that they were before a "man of God," who could speak on behalf of God. In a similar way, Origen recommends that sinners seek a competent healer for their suffering soul, one who can find the depth of their offence and propose appropriate remedies for the wounds and infirmities as a good physician does.[77]

Discernment – *diakresis*, illumination, saintly life and other qualifications of spiritual fatherhood, all these together gave credibility and in the course of history facilitated their recognition and veneration as true Church Fathers. It would be unfair to look only at their intellectual gifts. One more importance was their commitment to Christ's kingdom, their thought and work for his Church, and their efforts to make her a dwelling place of the Holy Spirit.

It is not only the acquisition of virtues and the building up of a true Christian life – a most laborious task, implying enormous sacrifices – but equally painful is the maintenance of such a precious life. The Church Fathers do not have any illusions, but they encourage fighters to remain watchful, alert, ready to face all the assaults of the enemy. This warning stems from the short admonition by St John, "Until I come, you must hold firmly to what you have. To those who win the victory, who continue to the end to do what I want, I will give the same authority that I received from my Father." (Rev 2.25-27). It is in such a spirit that St Theodore Studite advises a group in religious orders to keep their spiritual life under control to guard it from invisible enemies, above all from inactivity:

> Take heed from present realities, that every good is obtained only with a major effort. It can flee away easily if we do not remain attentive. That which was possessed after many years struggle, the least inattention and negligence can cause a loss. Be careful about yourselves in this present time, because it is now spring and the body now is full of life. Since our flesh is earthly, it demands that we behave according to the earthly conditions.[78]

Deeply conscious of their pastoral commitment and the commission mandated by Christ at their ordination, the Fathers are invested by the Holy Spirit with all that is constructive to replenish the missing elements within the members of the ecclesiastical body. They are not merely consultants, or advisers, but guides and spiritual fathers in the true sense. They know that this flock needs continuous nurture, guidance for growth, and a more accurate understanding of the Holy Scriptures, in order to solve the delicate and complicated issues which emerge in the healing of committed sins.

As is well known that when man comes into life, he is immature, ignorant, underdeveloped in spirit and in body. Bodily he is impotent to halt the aggressive elements in his nature and in the daily struggle to secure the means of a decent living. Even his spiritual powers lie dormant and are in an infantile and embryonic stage, waiting to be awakened and developed with the help of competent persons. Human growth follows a law of gradual expansion, step by step. Succor for his maturity and realization is an urgent inner need. Without help, he is often unable to overcome restrictions which impede his entry into a superior sphere. Of the ancient philosophers, first Plato rightly remarked, "Nurturing and *paideusis* – complete education which is virtuous and able to save, creates good natures."[79]

Of course, one must not neglect environmental and exterior factors. They are certainly important, and intervention from outside is needed. Is not the same said by St Paul concerning the messenger sent by God for salvation: "How can they believe if they have not heard the message? And how can they hear if the message is not proclaimed? And how can the message be proclaimed if the messengers are not sent out?" (Rom 10.14-15)

All the early ecclesiastical treatises, apologetic or didactic, during the persecutions and thereafter are nothing more than contributions of pastors intervening to clarify controversial issues, giving right directives and explaining the truthfulness of the faith, either to the neophytes or to those who are advanced in faith. In providing such admonitions, they express an established doctrinal or moral consensus, the conscience of the Church, so that nobody remains in doubts and ambiguity. Once accepted by the people of God, they silently gain authority and later councils will reconfrm their value.

From the earliest time, Origen reflects this practice in Alexandria. Shaken and worried by inner conflicts and thousands of queries, the faithful were seeking the right and sure directives. Origen asks them to be extremely careful in discerning the right persons for such important issues, those who can help them in providing the needed remedies, instructions and advice. Fallen in sin, they needed comfort and spiritual direction, from true physicians offering medical prescriptions for effective therapy and restoration.[80] Later, St Gregory the Theologian warned those who undertake such a healing ministry with so many grave responsibilities, to be exemplary, blameless, immaculate, so that they may be able to guide others towards God's pastures.[81]

If such are the requirements for acknowledging these distinguished persons in the Church as Fathers, and if their teaching is vital for a healthy spirituality in the life of the Church, what is also needed is human reception, endorsement and full cooperation. Christianity, then and now, has not been deprived of excellent fathers, teachers, guides, bishops, martyrs, saints, and confessors.

They are many, countless, like the innumerable stars. But Christianity is suffering and is weakened, because, although possessing so much patristic heritage and treasure, unfortunately their teachings are not being applied. Most of us agree with enthusiastic eulogies, admiring the depth and wisdom contained in what we call patristic writings, but we are not moving onward in their application or putting them into practice.

How often St John Chrysostom chastises his audience in packed congregations for its enthusiastic and spontaneous cheering applause? He complains that while the congregation is ready to confirm what has been heard in his edifying homilies, it is too lazy and quite unwilling to transfer those teachings into daily life, so that they may demonstrate how much they have been influenced. This just remark made by one of the most outstanding of the Church Fathers, reminds us of the bitter words pronounced by Christ against those Jews in Galilee who whole heartedly listened to his saving message, flattering him, but refusing to implement their essence in practice: "Not everyone who calls me 'Lord, Lord,' will enter the kingdom of heaven, but only those who do what my Father in heaven wants them to do" (Mt 7.21). Building up a complete personhood implies hard work from the educator. Thus, the Fathers never avoided harsh admonitions, calling black black. In our days our language has become too tepid.

In our modern society, plunged into fantastic superproduction, there is a systematic avoidance of certain key words. One hears less and less about evil, sin, death. In publicity on how to avoid AIDS, much euphoria is made of the ways and means of prophylaxis but we hear not a single word about avoiding the moral degradation from which such horrible diseases result. Confessors in such instances do not deal so much with cases and problems as with individuals. The whole scope of therapy is concentrated on a person's restoration to dignity. And here he must state loudly the unspeakable, what the world hesitates to speak of for our generation is antiseptic, already anesthetized and the sad reality meets with total indifference.

As evil invades our being, both the soul and the body are affected and contaminated. From that moment a collapse of the human system starts. As long as our spiritual and physical resistance are healthy, evil in whatever form appears will be attacked and driven away. A battle takes place. We avoid naming things for what they are, preferring vague, neutral and non-offensive terms, because AIDS is not a name – Acquired Immune Deficiency Syndrome – we prefer to use a signal. The disease has no name. Unnamed, faceless as death.

Chapter Nine

The Only Sure Guides for Understanding the Bible

There often appear complaints and sharp comments against Western theologians for their underestimation of patristic thought. However, this reaction from the Orthodox side, to a certain extent, may be true, nevertheless, we think that the blame equally applies to many of our faithful. Coming from different stands and traditions, both of them reach the same wrong attitude. For the Fathers, while maintaining the integrity of the transmitted apostolic faith, at the same time convey a commitment, a binding way of life contrary to the permissive life of this world. To such is the extent of the distortion that our age is known as post-Christian, and even de-Christianized. Even if the whole approach to the Christian faith by most of the Reformers depends exclusively on what is contained in the sacred text and nothing more, many of us do not go as deep, staying superficially on the exterior side of patristics, disbelieving their relevance for modern times.

Therefore, the question emerging for both is: How can we ignore the witness and experience of the past twenty centuries that is the historical dimension as to how millions of baptized lived our common faith? If we follow the development of Christian thought, we shall see that the Fathers are, in some way, on the historical line of interpretation, the first steps reaching us in the Scriptures, thus striking the continuity of its authentic interpretation throughout history, in the most tangible way. Nobody can dismiss and invalidate this continuity by bypassing these steps.

In many ways, the first Reformers did not intend to ignore patristics. Martin Luther or John Calvin often appeal to their voice, for they well understood that between the witness which the Scriptures render to Jesus Christ and the sixteenth century, there existed a whole history, what we call ecclesiastical history, of men and women, of confessors and martyrs, of the people of God. This reality of our fathers in faith cannot be thrown out just by a simple one-sided and hasty refusal. The Reformers were aware that in order to have a fruitful dialogue with the Holy Scriptures, the knowledge of the exegetic tradition was of capital importance.

After all, the history of psychology and philosophy has shown us the extreme importance of the past in the making of the life of men and of societies better and more meaningful. Man is a tributary of his past, not only becaise of his own personal past, but also because of the society in which he lives. Of course, if he wants, he is free to ignore the lessons and events of bygone times. But, then, this damages a fundamental principle of the human being, as a multidimensional creature, linked with his predecessors and preparing the way for the next generation. Should he free himself from any relationship with the past, he will become an isolated, misanthrope, separating himself from the entire human family. It is foolish Promethean behavior. Whatever he may do, he cannot escape his deep-rootedness to the past; the more he tries to be liberated from the past, the more he remains dependent, on it.

Similarly we may link the life of Christians into a process which consequently effects the whole life of the Church. Her members could, by ignoring her history, think that they are absolute, autonomous and perfectly free, free to read the Bible as they wish, free to apply it in so many complicated issues of life and proud that in doing so, they are in a direct dialogue with the sacred text. But in reality, since even the Bible in its present form depends on its past, that past in turn influences every new reader. All ethical norms and evangelical duties cannot be fully understood without turning our eyes on those who lived close to them, correctly and not disforming their true meaning. It is in this sense that the knowledge of the exegesis and its application in one's daily life through patristic eyes becomes indispensable, while ignoring their voice may lead us to unforeseen deviations and unpredictable disaster.

It is one thing to read the word of God, to try to understand its true meaning, but it is another matter how to apply it correctly, avoiding the extremes and sharp departures of the many heretical communities. This having been said, the role of the Fathers is comparable to the role of St John the Baptist. Last of the prophets, he ends the line of ancient Israel's witnesses. We have to pass through him when we leave the ground of the Old Testament in order to approach Christ. It is the same with the Fathers. We must pass through them in order to arrive at Christ and be acquainted with him. The outspoken affirmation by the Reformers of the fundamental authority of the Scripture, the *sola scriptura,* never sought disdain of the Christian tradition on the whole or of the patristic tradition. Thus, the Fathers connect us with the inner life of the old Israel and afterwards to the new, guaranteeing the continuity of the Church, a continuity liberated from ambiguous and unilateral interpretations, assuring a faithful view of Scripture and its revealed message.

A European scholar reflecting Calvinistic views, wrote a positive appreciation of patristic thought in 1632 in order to help the Protestants in Geneva in their reading of the Fathers. This author reflects the polemic spirit of the seventeenth century between Roman Catholics and Protestants, namely, whether patristics possesses authority or not. His imagery illustrates the extreme importance of the Fathers in enabling us, without prejudice, to see further than by our own efforts:

> Who knows not that a dwarf climbing on the shoulders of a giant, sees much higher and discovers much further than the giant. It will be ridiculous to conclude that what he saw has not been seen by the giant also. Nobody will accuse the dwarf of presumption, for what he saw for which the giant says no word or that the giant possesses the greatest part of dwarf's knowledge. This is what happens with us, the Protestants. They go up on the shoulders of this great and high antiquity. This advantage they gain from antiquity does not justify any presumption for what they were able to see because of this, since to antiquity we owe a great deal of what we have.[82]

We touch another point: namely, that in patristics one must not expect to find a critical scientific exegesis similar to that which was elaborated in the nineteenth century and which continues. Such research was not a priority for them and students will be disappointed. But exegesis has so many other very important aspects. The Fathers help us tremendously in finding the counterweight to the emptiness and spiritual poverty found in many modern commentaries which under the pretext of appearing scientific, strictly critical and historical pass over the fundamental dimension of our salvation in the Scripture. Today we are nearly twenty centuries distant from the New Testament authors, but the Fathers were much nearer to the salutary events and more competent to seize the spirit behind the scriptural records.

Consequently as St Irenaios of Lyons and Origen were not so distant from the New Testament authors, they participated in the same faith, the same piety and holy feelings; they possess the same sensitivity as the Apostles did. They are more apt to seize the key ideas and challenge the true meaning of the fundamental themes of the New Testament than authors of the twentieth century trained in the school of structuralism or rational criticism, thinking in different categories and animated by a quite different mentality. Of course, we do not suggest the exclusion of a critical exegesis, and there is no damage in an acceptable method of approaching the Scriptures. But it is very important to recognize that the patristic exegesis brings forth an indispensable corrective, indicating to us by a sure intuition the profound sense of the biblical text.

The exegesis of the Fathers allows us to understand how and why it is legitimate to proceed to a Christological exegesis of the Old Testament. The first Christians did not possess the New Testament. They possessed the Hebrew Scriptures inherited from the people of Israel. These writings represented for them the only written authority. What was more natural then to interpret this Old Testament in the light of the Christian revelation? It was natural for them to search in these writings as to how Christ, the accomplishment of the promises made to Israel, is already present in each page. For them, Jesus Christ was the key to opening the Old Testament. And this, again, did not have a meaning then, because it was the book announcing Christ, the book which did not speak anything else other than of Christ, the only book speaking of Christ.

In this context we should consider St Irenaios' *Demonstration of the Apostolic Preaching*. In this writing, the Old Testament is only invoked to justify the kerygma of the Apostles. In fact, the New Testament does not play a primary role here. St Irenaios is aware of this and writes:

> If one carefully reads the Scriptures, he will find there the word on the subject of Christ – *de Christo sermonem* – and the prefiguration of the new calling. He is indeed the hidden treasure in the field – the field in fact is the world – but in truth, the hidden treasure in the Scriptures is Christ. Because he is designed by types and words that humanly is not possible to understand before the accomplishment of all things, that is, Christ's parousia.[83]

That the understanding of the Bible is not an affair of intellectual research and critical investigation, but it is a mystery, is underlined by St Gregory the Wonder-worker (213-270), Bishop of Neocaesarea:

> Whoever claims to prophesy gift and one who listens, both need a grace. Nobody can listen to the prophets if the prophetic Spirit was not given to listen to these words. It is written in fact, in the Scripture that who closes, he also opens. It is the divine Logos which opens the closed things, by making intelligible the mysteries (Rev 3.7).[84]

Thus, this penetration into the mystery of the Scriptures is a gift of the Spirit, a grace coming from God, an action by Christ. Origen states this clearly:

> Let us beware also, because often we are near the well of living water, that is of the divine Scriptures, not be misguided for their approach....This is why, we need many tears and unceasing prayers in order that the Lord may open our eyes....But why use such a metaphor: to open the eyes? They are already open. Because Jesus came down to open the eyes of the blind and the veil of the Law was taken away.[85]

Further, the enormous interest in the patristics is seen in the vast field of dogmatics. The great doctrinal decisions taken by the Fathers in Nicaea in 325 during the controversy on the Trinitarian dogma and in Chalcedon 451 with regard to Christological ambiguities, maintain a vital place in our faith.

Firstly, their decisions possess a negative side. By rejecting without any compromise the heresies of that time, they demonstrate the mistaken ways of thinking advocated by theologians in every time. By condemning Arianism, the Nicaean Fathers show to us that every tentative effort to reduce Christ to the level of a created, thus minimizing his full and perfect divinity, is a most dangerous path to be avoided. By condemning again Nestorios, the Council at Ephesos in 431 shows us that both the divinity and humanity of Christ cannot be examined separately at the expense of the unity of Christ's personhood. The Chalcedon formula expressed in 451 shows us, inversely, that it is impossible to recognize the unity of the person of Christ at the expense of the duality of his natures. The permanent value of these conciliar decisions lies in preventing false solutions. Their actuality is to constantly remind us that "search" has its limits if we want to remain faithful to the revelation of the Scriptures. In fact, one can say, that the same tempting errors continue to appear before us, and we always need to be vigilant and prayerful.

The importance of the dogmatic statements by the Fathers has also its positive side. In fact, they locate, and also at the same time, limit the boundaries of any sincere study and scrupulous investigation or analysis of the great mysteries of our faith: the Trinitarian doctrine, incarnation, ecclesiology, soteriology, conciliarity, etc. Their writings are trustworthy, reliable, even deserving authority, because they reflect the infallible conscience of the Church throughout history. Most of current perplexing and agonizing problems, so delicate in their solution, were dealt with long ago by them. They knew what is essential and what is not. Modern students should remember that using a detailed, casuistic methodology, separating issues in groups and categories was not their way. They prefer a holistic, inclusive approach. By this, they invite us to be more humble, honest and not to think that we are the first to deal with this or that doctrine.

Rightly such saintly Fathers are named "dispensers" – *oikonomoi* of grace, celebrating the new and eternal sacrifice to God. St Dionysios the Areopagite will call them "celebrants of the sacred mysteries on the altar," and after that announcing and explaining them through preaching.[86] In the West, Leo the Great states, "The participation in the body and blood of Christ has no other effect than to transform us into what we receive,"[87] a reflection very dear to St Augustine, too.

Dispelling any exclusive intellectual or theological training as the supreme goal, we must point out the extreme importance of the Fathers in the field of pastoral care and the healing of souls. Their spiritual sensitivity, their personal experience of having tasted and lived the divine sainthood, makes them unique guides in this most difficult road towards evangelical perfection. St Dionysios the Areopagite was saying of his teacher Hierotheos: *"non solum discens sed et Patiens divina,"*[88] as having communicated by contemplation all that God can offer for our salvation. Relevant to this is what St Gregory the Theologian says in his first of five theological sermons concerning true theology: namely, the preparation by modesty, humility, inner purification, intensive prayer, and self-denial, if one wants to reach the mysteries of Christian faith. The same will be repeated by St Augustine, reminding us of the place of deep faith in a kind of living relationship with the Church, "only then theologians pious and truly spiritual" can advance in theological training.[89]

For the Fathers the task of theology is spiritual edification, warming the suffering heart. This moral process, often silent, astonishes all around them. Living in days when the majority of society was still pagan, they were a shining example. Most of them being converts, the newness of their extraordinary life was eivdence of the truthfulness of their faith. They spread in the scattered Christian communities in those days a missionary fever, an explosive vitality, a whole world of charity enabling these souls to act heroically in daily life and in their social contacts. It was this deep spirituality which motivated them to works of mercy, solidarity, helping the suffering, sick, widows, orphans, promoting woman's dignity, respecting the newly born, marriage fidelity and the charitable treatment of slaves. Their lives became the best evangelistic witness and missionary force.

The particular importance of and respect for patristics is due, for us the Orthodox, in order to secure strong ecclesiological spirituality. Growth in Christ is not an autonomous affair; it is the result of continuous paternal care by those being accepted as spiritual guides and Fathers. In the matrix of the body of Christ a relationship of persons is worked out. The Church, therefore, is not an institution with venerable rules and discipline. In physical life, life is transmitted from fathers to children through conception and birth. Similarly, the mystical life in Christ is communicated from the begetters to the newly born. The title "father" occurs in the most ancient texts, reflecting the principle of those who prepare their children, begotten in Christ, and further through them the grandchildren. When Joshua, son of Nun, "was filled with wisdom," a phrase indicating that he became leader of the people of God, the reason is given that "because Moses had appointed him to be his successor after having laid his hands upon him" (Deut 34.9). Clearly, here one sees the significant action of Moses as spiritual father for his spiritual child.

Later (9th cent. B.C.) Elisha the prophet in a most moving way asks to receive the prophetic charism from his spiritual teacher, Elijah, and to his surprise, he received it "twice," meaning in abundance: "Let me receive the share of your power that will make me your successor," Elisha answered: "You will receive it if you see me as I am being taken away from you; if you do not see me, you won't receive it," Elijah replied (4 Kg 2.9-10). Thus empowered, the successor of Elijah started a crusade against the religious and moral laxity of his time, especially the cult of Phoenician *baals* – gods. It seems that a major group was surrounding these two saintly persons. Elisha rent the fallen cloak of Elijah and retraced his steps. At the Jordan River, he used the cloak to part the water. Seeing this, the waiting prophets hailed him as the successor to Elijah and bowed down before him.

Such inspired spiritual guides know perfectly well that Christian ethics does not at all intend to make life unbearably complicated and more oppressive. On the contrary, Christ became one of us in order to help, by providing assistance to anyone caught in difficulties. Such a view obviously implies a certain flexibility, elasticity, capable of being easily stretched so that evangelical standards although demanding, become adaptable when needed, yielding to a certain point.

To remain intransigent, by refusing any moderation, overstating the uncompromising claim of God's commandments, we may fall into a rigid legalism, alien to Christ's mind. Such pliability was known even among ancient Greek philosophers dealing with delicate moral issues as seen in the following story.

We read of the philosophical method of Socrates (470-399 B.C.), going around the agora, the public market and discussing with ordinary craftsmen. By putting questions and analyzing their answers he was learning a lot, thus profiting from their experience and wisdom. This method is known as "maieutic obstetrics," eliciting new ideas from another.

One day Socrates stopped at the shop of a certain Pistias, an armor-maker of cork jackets to protect the breast. Socrates asked, "Why do people prefer your cuirasses than others, inasmuch as yours are not elegant nor luxurious?" The artisan answered, "Because I make them more resilient, manageable, easy to be bent without breaking, perfectly fitted to the body." But Socrates then put another question, "And what do you do if one's body is not well shaped?" Pistias answered, "I make these cuirasses well fitted to their bodies. Because one who knows how to manage the material becomes a skilled fitter, while the unskilled narrows the material thus becoming very tight." After having heard this Socrates concluded: "The best fitters are those who do not provoke grief to those in need fitting the wearer."

Chapter Ten

Tutors for Our Full Training and Growth

Already it was said the damages of misinterpretations, the effects from the dangerous raising of Arianism. Arius in reading the Bible arrived at quite opposite conclusions from his fellow countryman, Athanasios. How then, could both, reading the same texts, John 10.30 and John 14.9, reach such different understandings? The clue is that Athanasios, empirically living all the development of God's economy, was teaching that the Son of God came from the Father as very source of divinity, not in time but beyond time. He was not *created,* but *proceeded* in the eternal plan of God. Arius understood this procession in terms that there was a time when Christ did not exist and as happens in every birth, he came into being in time. Strangely, both used the same terminology but from different perspectives.[90]

A little later, the same linguistic problem was raised with Eunomios, a strict Arian-Anomian, concerning the relationship between the Father and the Son. St Basil was then making clear to his opponent (in 364) that in theology, first we conceive and specify a truth, and only afterwards do we try to find the appropriate words, the nearest possible. We are not allowed to manipulate a truth according to the words pronouncing it, but rather to fit language to the truth in question.[91]

If newly-born faithful confront enormous difficulties in their first steps, like babies physically unable to walk and to stand and therefore needing to be assisted and sustained by the helpful arms of their parents, similarly adults may be in the same situation of bewilderment and doubt. The mystery of our faith recorded in

Scripture, is often covered by a certain veil, grammatical, linguistic but above all spiritual. Philologists, historians, lexicographs, linguistic scholars can catch part of the very meaning, but only a poor portion, the rest remaining beyond reach.

Such difficulties emerged especially in the days of Origen. During this period of the third century, the climax of Origen's activities, one notes the influence of previous generations. There was a strong fermentation of ideologies, philosophical streams, opposing doctrines, a turmoil of religious and philosophical thought. An unexpected blossoming of mystic, esoteric, pseudo-apocalyptic ideologies, crypto-religious devotions inundating from Babylon, Asia, Persia, Egypt, Syria, Middle East, etc. In those days syncretistic worship was fashionable. The ancient mysteries of the Greek Eleusis, Samothrace, and elsewhere were in high demand.

The same phenomenon occurred among philosophers: all streams of thought were scrutinized either through curiosity or to finding out which was closest to the truth. But on what criterion was credibility to be given? Plutarch with his friends met together to discuss all the philosophical schools from Epikuros until Chrysippos. His treatise *ad Colotem* or *de Stoicorum repugnantiis,* witnesses a deep knowledge of intellectual matters. They investigate afresh the Stoics of those days, from Musonios to the emperor and philosopher Marcus Aurelius. Philosophy, one can say, ceases to remain the preoccupation of an elite few; it becomes the interest of all, because all are longing for something beyond this fragility of the earthly life. Thence, philosophy is popularized by its propagandists: Dion of Prusa, Maxim of Tyra, while Ammonius Saccas and Plotinos offer a new impetus to philosophical research.

Christians also are not idle between the second and third century. At the beginning of the third century, a number of outstanding Christian philosophers appeared. As such, we must qualify the classical Gnostics in this period: Basilides with his son Isidore, Valentinus with his numerous disciples, Ptolemy the Gnostic, Heracleon, Secundus, Marcion and Apelles. All these, although of Gnostic allegiance, still remain within the Church as members. And yet, they treat the greal problems of Godhead and his providence, the origin and the finality of cosmos, that of Christology and the relationship between an absolute God and cosmos, of redemption and revelation either of the Old Testament or the Logos, the Son of God.

The third century marks and highlights a growth of Gnostic sects of all kinds, detached from the Church and constituting rival or parallel movements, claiming to share all mysteries, while in the Marcionite sect their assembly becomes a rival church. In all these, as is attested by Hippolytus in his *Philosophoumena,* the fermentation of heterogenous ideas causes one to become puzzled. Expiatory rites, expectations, apocalyptic visions and revelations, syncretistic religions, directives for salvation, pseudo-asceticism accompanied with obscene practices: all are present at this meeting point, embellished with imagination and pseudo-science.

Among Christians there is a rapid emergence of new ideas. The apologists Aristides, Justin, Tatian become more and more productive in view of this resurgence of strange ideas. They continue the defense of Christian truth, following and opening the way for others such as St Clement of Rome, St Ignatios of Antioch, and the author of *Shepherd of Hermas.* With St Irenaios of Lyons and Hippolytus of Rome we see the appearance of the theology of interpretation of the Scriptures. Particularly, with Clement and Origen, both brilliant teachers in the famous Catechetical School of Alexandria, Christian thinking enters a most important era of exegesis. In brief, during this third century we distinguish four main streams: syncretistic religions, philosophy, Gnosticism and Christianity.

One may ask what in those days was the main problem for Christian thinkers? This question is related to the main characteristic of this rapidly changing period, namely, that it is dominated by a religious fever. In all social classes and religious groups, Jewish, non-Christian and Christian as well, religion absorbs the attention, while at the same time, the culture of antiquity still remains predominant. Thus, Epiktetos the Stoic, is taken in his writings by an astonishing spirit of mysticism. He speaks of God as if he were before him. Under different names, most of the thinkers treat what Christians also do, the Fall, redemption, Christ's saving incarnation, etc., with indirectly related Platonic, Stoic or Pythagorian views, which means that we find ourselves before a multifarious syncretism. Out of this emerged the system of Valentinus and of the other Gnostics.

The danger of distorting the true spirit of the Gospel was felt by the Church. Around 130, we see how the theology of St Paul, or the Logos of the Johannine Gospel were not totally well understood. Words and the language of the New Testament were not understood in the same way. The need for a prompt defense became evident. Christian language appeared strange, distant from daily realities. When a Christian used everyday language but inspired by Christ's kenosis, self-giving sacrifice, disdain of the earthly for God's kingdom, the outsiders were laughing in sarcastic irony, considering them as uneducated or unpolished. Thus, when Justin appears before the *praefectus urbi*, this high magistrate, is totally surprised at seeing such a learned Christian! The same case is repeated when, in the days of the Emperor Commodus, Apollonius (ca. 183-5) eloquently defends his faith before the judge Perennis and the Senate. His judges cannot understand how a cultured Roman aristocrat agreed to embrace the such absurd beliefs of Christians. Such widely circulating prejudices forced the most intellectual among Christians to formulate the faith in more elaborate philosophical language. Justin, Tatian and Athenagoras were involved in this.

Another pressing cause was that if Christianity wanted to reach the intellectual milieu, then it was indispensable to present the Christian message in a more literal and philosophical language. Converts who had been trained in philosophical schools, now started to use the same language to high intellectuals, friends or classmates. If they were in Athens, or Alexandria, or in Pergamon, they could only communicate in a language which was common and understandable to both parties.

St Clement of Alexandria was the first Christian able to catch the signs of the time. Residing in the great intellectual center of Alexandria, it was easy to see ways for fruitful and efficient canalization of the saving truth to non-Christians. In his famous Catechetical School, the composition of students determined the method of teaching: most of them coming from other philosophical schools, were longing for a higher message. The *Didaskaleion* was the ideal laboratory where he applied the *Paidagogos*, the unique, sure guide, not for knowledge so much as for building up a Christian life. Without neglecting the philosophical aspect, he reminds his selective audience, that the Catechetical School mainly seeks to educate the "true gnostics," that is, true Christians, equipped with the true science which will enable them to practice fraternal love.

His successor, Origen (b. 185), in his birth-place was surrounded by institutions feeding his encyclopedical training: the famous Museum of Alexandria with the two libraries, the studies of mathematics, astronomy, natural history, geography, disciplines established since the reign of the Ptolemean dynasty. Origen understood well that the exegesis of Scripture, by rendering both the letter and its spirit, was a priority task. He knew the contributions of the previous Gnostic exegetes, as Heracleon, author of the first commentary on the Gospel of St John. He knew Valentinus and Marcion equally well. His erudition was so well known, that Porphyry, a neo-Platonic, regretted that such a brilliant scholar was involved in a miserable delirium of quarrels between Jews and Christians.

Above all, Origen, reopening the School in 203 in a period of persecution, wanted to put as a priority the teaching of scriptural interpretation. His ambition was to make the *Didaskaleion* a biblical school. He refused to remain a simple commentator, but wished rather to develop the Christian doctrines. It was felt to be urgent to clarify the doctrine of God and his providence, in such a way that even followers of Plutarch could accept it. It was not enough to affirm faith in divine providence, in addition a philosophical demonstration was needed. Only in this way could he be accepted by his students who were rushing to listen to his courses. It is this aspect that led Origen to set out the Christian faith in the terms most fitted to Greek philosophy. It is this problem which he points out in the introduction of his *De Principiis:* "The holy apostles, preachers of the Christian faith, have transmitted to us in terms very clear that which they thought necessary to our faith; they left to those who deserved the eminent gifts of the spirit the care for providing the rational proof of their affirmations."[92]

At the end of his preface, Origen declared that what is needed is a body of doctrines and affirmations of the Christian faith, in the most accessible and intelligent form. Such a goal meets the will of God, who was made man in order to become visible, touchable and accessible. To Celsus, claiming that Christian teachers reach only old women, he replies, that on the contrary, that for educated listeners he teaches "that our beliefs are beautiful and come from God; but with regard to most deep teachings, they abstain from giving them to the simple since they cannot understand them"[93] Origen is aware that a teacher should adapt his language to his times. Avoiding any dialectic approach, he felt the need of a scientific and philosophical dress to the revealed truth. But such a delicate endeavor needed gifted, saintly, competent and charismatic guides, teachers and shepherds.

However great the importance Origen attaches to serious preparation and philosophical training in order to reach the very meaning of Scriptures he points out that without a saintly life and proper guidance by competent people and above all these the presence of God's Holy Spirit, the result will be very poor. Maturity in Christianity never springs from an autodidactic operation. God has appointed ministers, prophets and apostles to carry out this high task. Direct contact with the truth can never be guaranteed and obtained. To this end the Church with her ministerial functions and the catechetical process exists to feed young and adults, all continuously needing renewing knowledge inspiring dynamic forces.

Why is there such a persistent support for reading and relying on patristics? For many reasons. Mainly, because they are the privileged witnesses of the spirit, of the conscience and of the heart of the Church, this living body of the redeemed family of God. In the flow of the living tradition which continues throughout the ages from the very beginning of Christianity, the Fathers occupy a special place among so many other protagonists in the history of the Church. They are the first who labored on the architectural designs of the building from the gathered material; they formulated the doctrine against ambiguous circulating versions. They are the nearest to the purity of the origins of our faith. Some of them even witnessed the apostolic tradition, the very source from where the great river of our faith flows. In taking this precious material, they were able not only to preserve it unbroken and intact from any falsification and deviation, but even to develop and enlarge it, preserving the core and nucleus. As St Augustine rightly said: "They transmitted to us all that they have received. They have taught to the Church that they have learned within the Church. All that they found in the Church, they kept; that which they learned, they taught. That which they have received from the Fathers, they have transmitted to the sons."[94]

Chapter Eleven

Guides for Our Worship

When one day the disciples asked Christ, "teach us how to pray as John the Baptist taught his disciples" (Lk 11.1), they were reflecting a tradition among the Jews who often arranged their prayers and devotional life according to the instructions given by their priests. And this was legitimate, because communicating with the Almighty needs a certain amount of help and training. We do not have in mind here the spontaneous lifting up of our hearts to God in moments of despair or great suffering, but the regular liturgical life of the faithful who feel their insufficiency and need to be guided. While, therefore, prayer is a personal affair, its quality and efficiency depends on the appropriate guidance of godly persons.

The Church Fathers, with their wisdom and prayerful life, have given to the universal Church many tokens of their piety, in the form of liturgies, hymnography and various divine services. Even the texts of the sacraments are their inspired faith. The divine services used now are not the products of few professional theologians, as is sometimes assumed, but the result comes from the body of the worshiping community. Their authors are mostly anonymous, but reflect the prevailing feelings of wide congregations. This anonymity characterizes most of the early important treatises of ecclesiastical administration and directories on all possible important issues concerning the spiritual life of the people of God, such texts as *Constitution of the Twelve Apostles*, *Didache*, *Testamentum Domini – The Testament of our Lord*, *Didaskalia Apostolorum*, *Symbolum Apostolorum*, *Epistola Apostolorum*, *Apostolic Church Order*, *Canones Hippolyti* (c. 500), and many apocrypha. They were not meant to be literary works in the narrow sense. They were meant to offer and present a new meaning of life.

Today, scholars are puzzled in trying to establish the true authorship of these important documents offering us most valuable material for the discipline, religious life and liturgical particularities of our early brothers in faith. The Church Fathers in many ways preferred secrecy and anonymity, holding that they are instruments of God's love and care for his people. To these must be added a great number of unknown authors, coming from the grassroots of the faithful, who composed excellent texts. Conscious that worship is a joint venture of clergy and laity, not once per month but in daily life, they are marked by the conviction that they are the Church with its worship becoming their own inspiration and devotion – true *leitourgia* in the sense of being the work of the people, the liturgical assembly, the Church of God. Such liturgy is to be celebrated by all and for all. Whoever reads the history of the Church must not forget the universal or catholic dimension of the ecclesiastical body, embracing all cultures, all aspirations and reflecting every human need. Their composers inspired by the Holy Spirit knew not only the needs of those days, but even foresaw those of future generations, looking to the future with the prism of the present, a sort of ever-present living tradition. Filled with the sense of such responsibility, what they did was to be "now and forever, world without end, from ages unto ages," this classical expression concluding every liturgical prayer.

The authority of the liturgical rite stems and springs not from high institutionalized authorities, its form is not legislated, ordained, commissioned by officially established committees. Neither does it rely on official rigid constitutions dictated by superior officials and bodies. Neither does our worship come from the New Testament, as the Old Testament comes from rules of the Levitic ritual, or even from Ecumenical Councils. Our Divine Liturgy was born and developed, first unwritten and then written, in the very womb and life of the Church. Occasionally only synods and few councils dealt with specific liturgical aspects, offering solutions not by legislating anew, but by referring to an already existing tradition. Liturgical symbols, rituals, ceremonies, prayers, vestments, liturgical orders, altogether follow the living, ever-renewing reality of worshiping life, and they have as true origin liturgical tradition and order. St Symeon of Thessalonike (1429), who left us precious material of liturgical customs, recapitulates the leading principle of our worship: that order sustains all.[95] This view is extremely important, because, if one denies the close relationship between the innate thirst for the Other – Thou, with the shaped liturgical rite, then the whole liturgical theology is collapsed. The present content and shape of our worship, its very structure and rubric are not so much strictly determined either from any authoritative rules of the Holy Scripture, or from decrees elaborated by Ecumenical Councils, nor from pre-established norms. Its performance and practice on the other hand are not influenced from initiatives of individuals, however high their rank. Our worship is the expression of the whole life of the Church, it is the fruit of the prayerful communion with the Holy Spirit of the Church, of the liturgical experience. It is this coming together that embraces all manifestations in our life in Christ, reflecting the order of the celestial city in heaven. Rightly, the same St Symeon develops his thought: "Since the Church must copy the state in heaven, it needs order, a divine order and similar behavior."[96]

If we wish to have a more realistic view of patristics on the composition of liturgical texts, we must remember that the Fathers were living the faith in the worship and in the sacramental life. Their period was one of intensive liturgical elaboration. In the beginning, people were relying for the content of their *synaxis* mostly on certain Jewish liturgical traditions. Eucharistic worship developed in the early centuries step by step, with the appearance of tentative schemes, different but having in common the nucleus of canon, offertory, *anamnesis*, *epiklesis*. It is from such intensive labor that the great liturgies of the East and West emerged with inevitable ritual variations. What impresses us more is that this development is tied so closely with Scripture. It is always the Bible inspiring, dictating and providing the real background, to the point that one can say that our worship is an adaptation of Scripture. It suffices to look at the immense number of biblical quotations, or those which refer to a biblical text.[97]

This frequent reference has a double value. First, to acquire credibility by alluding to events which took place in the covenant of Israel in the Old Testament thence having a typological meaning prefigured there. Second, the sacraments were anticipated beforehand by certain symbolic events, thus indicating to us their significance. Let us take, as example, the eucharistic prayer of Hippolytus of Rome in the *Apostolic Tradition*. Its language is exactly the same as is found in the Bible:

> 'The Lord be with you' (Ruth 2.4); And all answer, 'And with your spirit' (2 Tim 4.22); 'Let us lift up our hearts' (Lam 3.41); 'We turn them unto the Lord' (Eph 5.20; Col 1.12; Rev. 11.17); 'It is right and just to do it' (Rev 4.11; Eph. 6.1).[98]

We find the same interchange of biblical words in the other groups of prayers in the early text of *Didache*.[99]

One can say that behind each word, phrase and each prayer offered or hymn chanted, there is a biblical resonance echoing the rich world of the Scriptures. The Fathers, by meditating on the word of God more than we do, were enabled by God's grace and specific commission to compose such set worship. In deep humility, shining in modesty, preferring to be little known, or totally unknown, they were, in their writing, followers of the example of St John the Baptist concerning the forthcoming Savior: "He must become more important while I become less important" (Jn 3.30). The liturgical corpus of the Fathers is a sign of their living solid love for God, shaped by the Bible and strengthened by its reading. Their distance from vainglory can be seen in the well known liturgies of St John Chrysostom, St Basil of Caesarea, St James, St Gregory the Theologian, the Presanctified Gifts, etc. They cannot be attested as coming directly from their hands, but rather they are products of a long process of work by unknown authors. The same can be said on many important patristic treatises, such as Pseudo-Dionysios, Pseudo-Makarios, Pseudo-Chrysostom, the high number of writings known as *spuria*, attributed to the authorship of a Father by unknown disciples, motivated by admiration and filial devotion. Modern critical scholars have gone to great pain to discover what is genuine and to identify the authoriship of these works.

The Orthodox Church has retained this liturgical tradition related to the Fathers, and because of such close links, she is nearer to the Bible than some Reformers might think. By maintaining this continuity and line, she is able to draw all necessary forces and its usefulness in the Bible. Unfortunately, such was not the case for the churches that came out of the Reformation. The sixteenth century brutally broke the bridges with the past and the liturgical tradition, resulting in a terrible impoverishment of liturgical life and practically reduced it to a desert. There is a gap which isolates us from the great stream of life emanating from the primitive Church and which prevents us from having access to the Scriptures. Certainly, this was not done deliberately. Luther had well transcribed the Roman Mass in German,[100] but carried away by extremists and the whole polemic climate he reached unexpectedly radical conclusions.

The same may be said of John Calvin who filled his Geneva liturgical text with ecclesiastical sacramental terms.[101] But under pressure of time and due to the unusual circumstances he did not realize his project. His liturgy does not look like either the worship of the early Church or the liturgical life of the growing post-apostolic period. Unwillingly, the Reformers went too far. They cut off their communities from the most reliable reference to the Scriptures represented in the liturgical tradition of the patristic period.[102]

Another point needs to be stressed, namely, that by producing liturgical texts patristic tradition played a great role in expressing the immense wealth of the Scriptures, the source of their inspirations. If the Church holds that Christ would never abandon her until his return, she cannot ignore this innermost tradition. By emphasizing the Fathers' value, she manifests the existing unity of the Church throughout all places and all times. Any change or modification in worship must take into account this unbroken liturgical tradition. By offering more space to the liturgical products of the Fathers, a modern ecclesial community will again find its place in the great stream of spiritual life. Then, it will also again find the sense of continuity in history and in time, with parallel achievement, rediscovering the unity, the catholicity and oneness.

It is known that in the early period some heretics tried to exclude the Old Testament from their worship; such were the Gnostics and Marcionites. But the Fathers immediately understood the great danger of this. The risk was of making the Gospel an intemporal myth and thus to fall into docetism, a tendency which considered the humanity and sufferings of Christ's manhood as apparent rather than real. They were wise enough to keep the sense of continuity in the history of salvation, the sense of revelation by God in the course of history. They strove to conserve its books intact by vigilant and scrupulous diligence. Since then, and thanks to the Fathers' stewardship, two dimensions of the Old Testament were jointly conserved: the historical dimension, called by Origen "the letter," and the Christological dimension, that is the spiritual and ecclesial. At the school of the Fathers we learn the importance of these two aspects of the Old Testament.

Briefly, the content of worship was not set up by specialists and then imposed upon the congregation. This would be against the essential right of religious liberty. Rather, it is the fruit and spontaneous expression of a long process of devout feelings in the worshiping community, the last stage being shaped by the Church Fathers.

The spiritual growth and vivification of the baptized for patristics is realized in the frame of the Church's ministry of sanctification and Christian worship. This consists of liturgical services, enabling the faithful to reach the living Triune God, and especially to participate in the mystical life of Christ. Consequently, worship contemporizes what is considered as the past. The past becomes actual, present, *hic et nun*. Thus, the life and the work of Christ as a living reality are transmitted and renewed to each believer and, consequently, to the whole congregation, in each local community. By the *anamnesis* we commemorate past events, like the Passion and Resurrection of Christ. But by the *epiklesis*, we have in a mystical way these events again before us. The Holy Spirit transcends time and space and thus throughout the liturgical year we share the great events of Christ's life, as well the lives of his saints. This liturgical experience helps enormously in the creation of a true living spirituality in Christ. Our life follows and is identified with the life of Christ. As St Gregory the Theologian said: "To be buried with Christ, to be risen together with Christ, to be co-heirs with Christ, by becoming son of God, even to such a degree as be god – *theon auton.*"[103]

Eucharistic worship does not simply seek a periodical alimentation, only a ritual distribution of an established sacrament. If we take worship as the mere duty of church-going and attending a demanded office, then it naturally becomes a static thing. Worship seeks personal union with Christ, having first purified our soul from all iniquities through repentance and prayer. Christ seeks the metamorphosis of all our being and the world together, to shape our life according to God's will. St Gregory of Nyssa brietly described the aim of Christians: "Christianity is the copying of the divine nature."[104]

Behind almost every term, every phrase of this prayer one finds an allusion, a Biblical echo. Indeed, the liturgy for the Fathers is none other than the expression of a profound piety, awe and communion of the worshiping soul, shaped by Scripture and fed from its reading. After all, there is no one single service, sacramental or not, where there are no readings from the Bible. In the early liturgical practice, there were three or four such readings from the Old Testament, from the Gospels and from the Epistles, followed by an edifying homily, usually given by the bishop presiding over the liturgical assembly.

In composing liturgical texts, Sts Gregory, Basil, James, Chrysostom and others were focusing on the real goal of theology, becoming doxological. At the same time, they were taking into account the aspirations and particularities of a local church. They were expressing the content and the form of the liturgy within the concrete society where they were living, so that the worship could be seen as their personal prayer, and not a foreign one, imposed from outside. They were thinking in terms of the Greco-Roman culture, borrowing from Hellenistic symbolisms which could be used for the worshipers. Thus, they show us the necessity, but also the limitations, of adaptation. If often in these texts one finds abundant Trinitarian theology and doctrinal expressions, this is because the Fathers through the liturgy had to defend the Orthodox faith, but also through the same liturgy, to teach the faith, to educate, and to shape character. Indeed, liturgy is also an efficient pedagogy, by offering the lives of martyrs and saints as a model and stimulus for encouragement and imitation.

It is not surprising, therefore, that the Fathers were earnestly preoccupied with the composition of liturgical texts, with improving and enriching them and on liturgical renewal. How many liturgies and eucharistic anaphoras are associated with their authorship, though in humility the authors systemically avoided using their names?

The whole liturgical setting, with its doctrinal hymnography, helps the worshiping community to attain a profound penetration into the mystery of the incarnation and the communion with Christ. Thus, in the feast of Christ's Nativity the ceremony begins with a joyful hymn (attributed to St Germanos, Patriarch of Constantinople): "O come, let us rejoice in the Lord, as we declare this present mystery." This hymn deals with the ineffable mystery of the reconciliation of man with God, the relationship broken by man's fall. But now, when the infinite mercy and philanthropy of Christ comes to man, the wall of disunion between creation and the Creator is destroyed, the flaming sword of the Cherubim is turned back, clearing the way to the Tree of Life. Thus, man acquires access to the fruits of the former Eden which the first man possessed before the Fall. Herein lies true spiritual joy which signifies the first manifestation of the vital forces in man after he tastes the fruit of Paradise. The fruit of the Tree of Life gives light to those who taste it: "When the Lord Jesus was born of the blessed Virgin, the whole creation was lighted."[105]

"O Christ our God, Thou hast enlightened us byThy coming. O Light of Light, O Radiance of the Father,Thou hast illuminated all creation; and every breath does praise Thee, the Image of the glory of the Father. O God who are and who has ever been, Who has shone forth from the Virgin, have mercy upon us."[106] As is evident from this hymn, an unusual transformation takes place throughout the creaturely world by reason of the Incarnation. With it, the material world becomes a participant of the divine life. The author of such change is O ¿N , Jehovah, "He who exists," eternally alive, the living One and who alone is the source of life in the world, and who is fulfilling the promise made to our forefathers, to Moses on Mount Horeb in the words "I am who I am" (Ex 3.14). Christ's epiphany reveals his close relations with the whole universe. Through the Nativity on earth " he who is" becomes most closely connected to, and committed to, God's creation.

The light and joy of everything that exists will be eternal, because the kingdom of Christ is the kingdom of all ages, its power extends to all nations and the great powers of the Gold, Silver, Bronze and Iron Ages will serve as an instrument to the divine providence in the salvation of man. It is generally believed that Cassia the hymnographer (9th c.) composed a hymn which recapitulates the whole history of salvation thus by the Incarnation bringing to the whole humanity hope, joy, peace and consolation:

> When Augustus reigned alone upon the earth, the polyarchy of men came to an end; and when Thou didst become incarnate of the Pure One, the polytheism of idols was annulled. Under one earthly sway were the cities, and in one dominion of the Godhead did the Gentiles believe. By the command of Caesar were the people inscribed; and we faithful have been inscribed with the name of the Godhead, of Thee our God, who hast become man. Great is Thy mercy, O Lord, glory to Thee.[107]

Thus, we are before a continuous concern of God for his children. Indeed, our God is *Kyrios*, or in Hebrew, *Eloha*, *Elohim*, *Adonai*, and the tetragram YHWH, the most sacred proper name of God of history, considered as ineffable and none dared to pronounce it. We know that the revelation of this proper name of God was made after the episode of the burning bush when God answered to Moses concerning his question about the divine name, "Elohim said to Moshe: '*Ehie asher ehie*' " (Ex 3.14). This confirms the engagement of God to carry on his active providence, to draw the alienated world to its very source and to the Creator.

Ekklesia – from *ek-kalo* – implies an exodus of one from his traditional milieu and way of life, to another style of existence. Thence, he becomes not one of the many, but one unusual, distinctive, an ecclesial person, member of the Body of Christ, visibly seen as a different being. Certainly human, but at the same time beyond human norms and standards. Thus, the parishes were something distinct according to Greeks and Jews. The marks and signs of such distinctiveness were formulated officially in credal texts. The addition made by the Second Ecumenical Council of 381, "I believe in one, holy, catholic, and apostolic Church," to the short formula of the First Ecumenical Council of Nicaea in 325, "I believe in the Church," reflects also existentially the daily conduct of its members. Here are found the marks of the local parish and of each parishioner as well.

God wants the redemption of the entire human family, seeking to bring together all races, nations and human beings into one community. Thence the importance of human relations. Every eucharistic worship invites the worshiper to go out and cultivate relations outside with others around him, bringing them to God. This action takes many forms. We often speak of the "liturgy after liturgy." In short, man acquires value the moment he gets out of his restrictive and exclusive self, by entering into personal relationship. In modern language "relation" is a vague expression. What is meant by relation in the ascetic language, is a self-giving process, with due respect for the needs and personal integrity of the other. Parish, in the ecclesiological sense, becomes the workshop for such edifying relationships, communication and communion. Only there one learns what "brother" and "sister" mean.

How the Fathers understood the Church risks remaining an unanswered question unless we actually live their own experience and place ourselves in the context of their inquiry. For them, the Church is a living personal experience. Each member is, therefore, an ecclesial being, committed, engaged to incarnate the values and the marks of the Church in his life. Thus, he confirms what he is, to where he belongs. He identifies his life with that of the Church, of Christ. He never offers a definition of the Church; *he becomes himself a church.* And he repeats to the pagan persecutors, as the martyrs: "I am Christian," thus proclaiming that for him life and death is to belong to, and to live the qualifications of the Church and its head, Christ.

Liturgical worship and the eucharistic life becomes the central focus of their aspirations and daily life. Apollos, one of the early ascetic Fathers, states:

> The monks should, if possible, partake of Christ's mysteries every day. He that remains away from them, draws away from God; but he that partakes of them, receives the Saviour constantly. For the saving voice says, 'He that eats my flesh and drinks my blood, abides in me and I in him.' This, then, is of benefit to the monks keeping the rememberance of the redeeming Passion faithfully, and being ready every day by preparing themselves to be always worthy of welcoming the heavenly sacraments.[108]

This frequent communion must not be taken as a blind observance of strict rules imposed by the constitution of a community, but rather as a consequent commandment of Christ's will to remain in intimate communion forever with his members. Each one, therefore, needs to refuel his soul with Christ's communion materialized in the eucharistic fellowship. Especially those engaged in spiritual intensive warfare need enormous resources and renewed strength to preserve their spiritual integrity and to march in their day by day ascension in Christ.

Chapter Twelve

A Case Study

One of the many difficulties early Christians had to face was to discover the meaning of the sacred texts. It is one thing to have before you in written form the word of God, and another to be sure that this is the true rendering. The same words currently spoken were used even by non-Christians, but understood according to their philosophical conceptions or pagan background. Between a quarreling married couple the same words which are exchanged have for each partner a different meaning, and this is what divides and provokes deplorable conflicts. Pre-Cappadocian Fathers were drawing the attention of intellectual converts to how the meaning of philosophical terms used by Plato, Aristotle and others, although being accepted by the Christian language, were conveying quite different things. For instance, St Athanasios of Alexandria was fighting Arians precisely on this language problem by showing that what counts is not the exterior grammatical shape of a word, but its profound meaning – *ennoiai*. Much confusion was spread in those days due to the linguistic problem, that perplexed and frustrated Christians who were waiting for a guidance and authoritative pronouncements. And, then, the true exegesis of biblical texts by the Fathers finally brings security, relief, peace and gratitude. There are many instances the Fathers admit the existence of "deep clouds" of "desperate darkness," but guided by the Holy Spirit gave an end to doubts, uncertainties and poisoning frustrations.

St Gregory the Wonder-worker (d. 270), leaving Caesarea of Palestine, the fervent disciple of Origen, delivers in 238, on the day of his departure, a panegyric to his great teacher – *didaskalos*.

Among other things, he reveals the exegetical approaches and techniques used by Origen in order to unveil the darkness and obscurity of biblical texts. Origen's competence was seen as one who sees the agony, rushes to help one tired and exhausted by a long walk. If one meets in a difficult text ambiguous phrases, doubtful and misleading, he was offering a hand for salvation to one risking to be drawn in water.[109] Purposely the Bible contains such difficult texts in order to challenge readers to develop their unexploited resources and eagerness for learning, turning to God's guidance through the appointed saintly teachers. St Gregory admits in humility, that driven away from the school, he has forgotten to listen to the true exegesis, due to the time past and because the texts belong to bygone days, with the results becoming unclear and obscure. Origen's intervention much helped by clarifying and bringing all to the light. But the function of such a teacher, as for every true teacher – *didaskalos*, is not restricted to solving enigmatic sentences like a crossword puzzle, but is more sacred and substantial. Namely to inspire God's friends and prophets and unveil every prophetic truth, mystical and divine word and consequently, after having investigated and found out the meaning of the words, to understand in the true sense, to believe and the most important, to follow God, this being the climax of any true research.

We offer below, a portion of this important speech by St Gregory, reflecting not only the deep respect to his teacher, but equally, the charismatic privileges God bestows on chosen saintly souls:

> All that Origen was teaching – in the Catechetical School – I presume was due to the communion he had with the Holy Spirit. And this is needed by both the prophetising and those listening to the prophets. For one would not be able to hear a prophet if it were not granted by the Spirit to him the gift for understanding his words. Such is the meaning of even the words found in the sacred writings. 'And he shall open, and none shall shut; and he shall shut, and none shall open' (Is 22.22 and Rev 3.7). Indeed, the divine word discloses what is hidden by signifying what is enigmatic and obscure. Origen acquired this highest gift from God, and, on the one hand, the most brilliant potentials from heaven being assigned as interpreter of God's words to men, by making man to understand in such a way, as if God himself were speak-

> ing, and, on the other, narrate to men as men are able to listen. Consequently, nothing now remains unspeakable, neither hidden or impenetrable. It became possible to learn every discourse, be in Greek or in other barbarian (language), of mystical nature or of political, either divine or human, with much boldness investigating and scrutinizing all, eager to catch everything, enjoying the resulting goods of the soul. Whatever name one could give to them, either lesson of the old truth, we were there present, for preparation and full acquisition of the most wonderful visions.
>
> And summing up, this man – Origen – was for us a true paradise, copying that great paradise of God. It was not meant to work in as an earthly one, nor for feeding our body. But only striving how to promote the benefits of soul, as if we were planting ourselves beautiful plants, or rather, these plants being implanted by the very Author of all in us, for our enjoyment and gratification.[110]

Love for patristics does not mean the accumulation of quotations from the Fathers in texts in order to show the serious attention given by an author, but rather how to interpret their thought to current new situations. It is a terrible manipulation by a few who, by presenting long patristic texts, often irrelevant or very weak, think that they demonstrate their faithfulness to the early tradition. We have to work as they did, considering all emerging issues, analyzing them in the light of the Gospel and then in humility conclude with relevant stimulating reflections. If our contemporary problems are the same and the expected solutions seem identical, the answers vary because of the passage of time, the developing situations and new directions in our society. The answers of the past need to be reshaped, re-elaborated and take the garb of the present times. We must proclaim the same truth, but placing it in a current context. It suffices here to mention the contents of Karl Barth's monumental work, *Kirchliche Dogmatik,* in order to see the extent and the place given to the Church Fathers in a modern, extensive work of dogmatics.

If today the notion of contextual and indigenization are so important for the acceptance of Orthodox Christianity in the Third World, or even in this secularized and desacralized society, then we must follow the example of the Fathers. They had to face the

Greco-Roman culture and in this environmental reality all their arguments, language and approach were fitted to these challenges. Heralds of the Gospel, they were trying to express it in the framework of the Hellenistic culture, by retaining certain useable, positive elements and by rejecting negative ones. Adoption, therefore, implies flexibility, wisdom, a selective approach, not throwing out the baby with the bathwater. In this respect, patristic wisdom can give enormous support to missionary activity in modern times, helping us to avoid our identification with Western culture.

The same may be said concerning the defensive attitude toward modern sects and heresies. Error has always been the same, but with certain variations. Modern heresy in whatever form, tries to amputate the Gospel from this or that element, by overstating this or that aspect, or by introducing a kind of minimalism, relativism or syncretism. Such streams can be identified in the so-called uncontrolled radical charismatic movements, illuminationists, sectarians, integrists, neo-gnostics who are borrowing ideas even from Asiatic religions. There is no modern heresy which cannot find its roots to the past and confronted by the Fathers. How did they succeed in overcoming all these threats?

By always referring to the unbroken continuity of the faith and spirituality guaranteed in the genuine membership in the Church. Again, since this Church is not an amorphous body but is hierarchically structured, the appointed *episkopoi* are vigilant in discerning the measure or the excessive on the border of Christian behavior. Since what it means to be a Christian cannot be established in strict and precise terms, most of the determining conditions and guidelines were not transmitted in written form. At the heart of this reference lies the idea of the ecclesial fellowship – Plato preferred his ideal city – and to certain critics this may appear anachronistic, too often invoking the past. But we must not forget that for the Fathers, our roots, remain in the ground of the Church family, as in a vessel. For it is in an unceasing sailing through turbulent waters of the sea. The captains are to navigate the ship, watching to what direction the wind blows and consequently how to use the sails and oars. Winds may change rapidly and prompt action is needed, otherwise accidents may occur.

Long before the formulation of the canon of the New Testament, oral preaching was the only channel for the transmission of the truth. This was invested with full authority, uncontestable, and the Church was built up on this oral tradition as the only authority. But with the codification of the canon, another difficulty arises: how to interpret it, how to relate the inherited oral tradition to the written Scriptures, how to reconcile the authority of the Scriptures and the authority of tradition. It is remarkable how the Fathers offered solutions to such controversial issues and most thorny questions.

Chapter Thirteen

How to Treat the Heterodox

Although from very early times Christians were seeking, both during worship and in private prayers, the correction and repentance of those who had broken with the ecclesiastical fellowship, in reality the human contacts between orthodox and heterodox were not easy. How to treat them, how to converse or even to greet them in daily life? Still today, there is a certain embarrassment and confusion in finding appropriate language for dealing with schismatics, heretics or non-Christians in spite of the attachment to ecumenical fellowship. And because of such difficulties, the meeting with them, communication through honest dialogue, and the willingness to help them are hindered. In writings and speeches it is not infrequent to find the use of unfriendly expressions, humiliating adjectives and insulting words against non-Orthodox.

But such an attitude and hostile behavior lead to their isolation, alienation from our communion, resulting in irritating and hostile feelings. And in all this, where is our charity? What is missing in such a disdaining relationship is our complete absence of not only elementary flexibility and diligent behavior, but also the conviction that in spite of such divergence, they do not cease to remain children of God, icons of God. There is no justification for our unfriendly stand, for offending with the most cruel words, and even refusing to address them as "brothers."

In this respect, what is the attitude of the Fathers? There are numerous instances in which they declare that they do not hate sinners or heretics, but only sin and heresies. Rather, they are indulgent and charitable towards the weak and erring, encouraging contacts and efforts for honest dialogue and final reconciliation.

But this implies a constructive psychological climate which will be created only by avoiding harmful and humiliating language. In Church history, we meet examples of such mildness and gentleness, a main characteristic of saintly persons. By adopting such an attitude, errors were defeated and truth returned to its throne. However, we also find polemic, anti-Jewish expressions sometimes partly due to pressing imperatives during persecutions.

From the many examples, we propose one most significant, that of Dionysios of Alexandria. In 251, Novatian, a distinguished presbyter in Rome, came into conflict with Cornelius, the Bishop of Rome. Their difference was the problem of those who had offered sacrifices during the persecution of Decius (249-251); how should they be treated since sacrifice to pagan idols was considered a mortal sin? Cornelius was indulgent to human weakness and accepted their reconciliation upon proofs of their true repentance. Novatian not only refused such an approach, but even rose up against the leniency of the bishop, thus creating an integrist radical group, competing in some way with the official ecclesiastical body. The situation worsened and nearly to the point of an openly schismatic church hostile to any re-admission to ecclesiastical communion, thus challenging the charitable policy practiced by Cornelius.

At this critical time, Dionysios of Alexandria (247-265), motivated by brotherly feelings, intervenes. This was the practice of mutual solidarity between sister Churches, when a bishop was expected to offer his good offices; he then writes to Novatian a very short letter pleading for reconciliation and a return to peace. Dionysios, a disciple of Origen, an outstanding ecclesiastical writer and peacemaker, in a most reconciliatory style asks the rebel presbyter to restore the broken communion with his bishop, as is also attested by Eusebios the historian.[111] What impresses us in this context is that Dionysios calls Novatian "brother" – *adelphos*, considering him in spite of all a valid brother in Christ. The whole text in its shortness reveals Christian feelings and wisdom.[112]

Thus, Dionysios shows the way to treat opponents to Church order and discipline. In the same lenient spirit he writes to Fabius, Bishop of Antioch, asking to receive the repenting.[113] Later he informs Stephen, Bishop of Rome, that the division was healed and that throughout Christendom there prevails joy and peace.[114]

Certainly the Fathers were well aware of the severe warnings by

Christ against close association with erring persons, advising us to keep our distance and in some way breaking down relations and fellowship:

> When you come to a town or village, go in and look for someone who is willing to welcome you, and stay with him until you leave that place. When you go into a house, say 'Peace be with you.' If the people in that house welcome you, let your greeting of peace remain; but if they do not welcome you, then take back your greeting. And if some home or town will not welcome you or listen to you, then leave that place and shake the dust off your feet. I assure you that on the day of judgment, God will show more mercy to the people of Sodom and Gomorrah than to the people of that town! (Mt 10.11-15)

> Avoid stupid arguments, long lists of ancestors, quarrels and fights about the Law. They are useless and worthless. Give at least two warnings to the person who causes divisions, and then have nothing more to do with him. You know that such a person is corrupt, and his sins prove that he is wrong. (Tit 3.9-11)

The excommunication implicitly described here is clear. The erring or heretic must be ignored and banned. But such an attitude may even go too far and create a fanaticism, a hate, even persecution. If contacts are not allowed with him, people overpassing the spirit of such warnings may condemn the person in question into a total exclusion of human relationship. The deeper implication of such attitude must be seen in the intention for his correction, and eventual return to the family, the Church. Exclusion, therefore, has a rather reformative and corrective character. The guilty must become conscious of his misdeed, to express contrition of heart and consequently to return to the communion. Origen disapproves of the use of violent acts against the erring brothers.[115] St John Chrysostom states that learning the true faith does not imply use of violence, because Church ministers are not authoritarian despots forcing the flock to obey, but rather helpers, advisers, spiritual fathers seeking in charity to make the true faith acceptable.[116]

St John Chrysostom, defending the Christological faith on

Christ's full divinity and humanity against the Anomeans, often treats this subject as to how to face heretics in general. He is not aggressive, but rather recommending elasticity and willingness to regain their confidence, by reintegrating them into full ecclesiastical communion.[117] To be cautious towards heretics does not exclude considering them as our brothers. What is detestable is not sinners, but sins. On this basis is established the principle for a just and balanced attitude to all kinds of heterodox:

> We undertake a long run fight full of indulgence and sweetness in order to remove the heretics from death to the life, helping them to stand up. We are fighting not against the heretics but chiefly against heresy. Not against a man, but against errors. Myself, I am engaged in fighting heretics, but my intention is not against these men I fight, but striving to remove from them the error and heal rottenness.[118]

Such being the very root of our divisions, if one accepts the non-exclusive spirit of many ecumenists, precisely because of this great respect between different confessional families, one could fall into the opposite trap of exclusivism and fanaticism, that is to say, a superficial, "unsalted" Gospel. That by not offending the different creeds becomes reduced to an attitude of limited depth in the very truth of the undivided faith, and up to a certain point we cannot avoid to acknowledge this. This is why, in many meetings, on proposing the theme some try to avoid unhappy disagreements, all that could be a means of depth or that could give rise to sharp divergences. Such a minimalistic approach can be compared to two people that for some time had been enemies because of grave reasons, and that as the years pass had gradually become more tolerant and cordial, up to the point that they are capable of greeting each other, meeting from time to time to talk. However, total and true reconciliation will not be achieved until the motives of the ancient quarrel are acknowledged and brought out to the light. Only in this way will a true reconciliation be achieved.

In an ecumenical relationship, in the Church Fathers' mind, if the differences in doctrine are not touched on because of the fear of hurting it and culminating violently, certainly then we may have very fraternal meetings. All this is very good and the fruit of friendly contacts, but as a consequence of it, we fall into this "de-salted" faith that was already mentioned above. Unity negotiations thus compromised, will only advance if, with a spirit of authentic humility, renouncing all fear, the roots of disunity which continue to be great are driven out, realizing that they are not only questions of language and style as some believe.

As Orthodox, we have spent many decades talking of union, of the coming closer of all, to try to solve, once and for all, this paradoxical situation in which we, the children of God, find ourselves. What has happened? What impediments are there that slow down, put on the brakes or defeat the magnificent desires of all Christians who are truly anxious to protect ourselves in the divine shelter of the one and only God?

Everybody who intends to integrate themselves into the family of the sons of God, has to start by renouncing many of the things carried inside that from time to time surface so that others may see our qualities and by so doing acquire this first place of honor that we all like so much and, without often realizing, desire with all our hearts. The light of God's Spirit is what clarifies the road leading to a real and effective communion.

The deafness of our selfishness stops us from hearing Christ's call to reconciliation. A strong final knock on our hearts will be necessary so we can awaken from the stupor in which we find ourselves and listen to the delicate voice of Jesus, knocking at the door of our dwellings, saying to us: "This night I will eat with you." Christ is in the entrance porch of each house waiting to enter and to offer us reconciliation.

In point of fact, there is no written uniform attitude towards non-Orthodox. It varies according to existing local situation and the specific emerging issue. After all, a stereotyped list of precepts and answers does not exist. Those ignorant of the holistic approach contained in Orthodox ethics and thinking in casuistic terms, feel that many of the existing but irrelevant answers are all too stereotyped and devoid of substance. Many Christians would probably feel they were better understood if there were a Church ministry which first of all trained them to do that which most of them have probably never learned or forgotten over the course of time. The absence of detailed guidance causes many to think of the Church as a gigantic, overblown apparatus, kept going by innumerable clergy, an organization where searching after God and the truth seems to take second place. But what happens really here is that people misunderstand the Church from its earthly aspect, forgetting that her members are charismatic with full responsibility to contribute, to take initiatives, creative, and by prayer, spiritual advice and reading the Scriptures to fnd out the right solutions.

Conclusion

Warnings launched fifteen centuries ago are still relevant today, inasmuch as three dangers threaten the future of humanity. 1) Man has always been capable of killing his neighbor. Now with nuclear weapons, he is even able to exterminate his own species. Millions of species of animals and vegetables have disappeared. 2) Man was capable of shaping nature for his proft. Delivered to himself, he can destroy the ecological environment which so much helped the presence of life. In other words, he is capable not only to destroy his species, but all species together, too. 3) Lastly, man was capable of triumphing over sicknesses. Now with genetic engineering, he is in a position to infiltrate and intervene to exclude beings destined to be invalids or seriously sick or, according to arbitrary criteria, destined to become weak or useless.

These three remarks for the eventual ruptures may seem sufficient to produce dizziness, many of us becoming mad. The progress of technology and the adventures or acrobatics of our intellect can conceive the most terrible calamities against his own interest and the interest of others. Any moment we risk the most unimaginable genocide. Hate dominates between those who possess everything and those, more numerous, who have nothing. Can we anticipate the day when the atomic bomb will be used against, let us say, multitudes of hungry and needy inundating our Western society?

However much credibility patristic wisdom can obtain, objections may still appear from some contemporaries, mainly because of their distance and the seemingly new events appearing in the course of history. The argument is that humanity is in a continuous process of evolution, changes touching all aspects of human life. Consequently, new phenomena are emerging and need new investigations and different interpretations and pronouncements. If this is so, then we have to question the existence of permanent and everlasting values and criteria.

Briefly, we have to emphasize that the Fathers are not concerned with details, with epiphenomena, but with the essentials of phenomena. Certainly, we cannot find absolute uniformity in all matters discussed; there is a certain difference in expression and exterior manifestations, due to socio-cultural developments. Our food, our dress, our daily manners have since changed, but what is permanent in phenomena is their substance, the nature, therefore parallelism and analogy are permitted. Thus, the Fathers are not interested in forms and secondary syndromes, but in roots, substantial causes and their immediate effects on human personhood. What, then, was essential as food, is also so today. Avidity, vain glory, sensuality, egoism, luxury, and the opposite, humility, self-denial, eternity, hunger for deep spirituality, inner conflicts, thirst for the Other – Thou, etc., to mention only a few, constitute permanent, serious and vital issues, needing competent diagnosis and consequent treatment.

Thus, the Psalmist, speaking on behalf of God asks: "How long will you people insult me? How long will you love what is worthless and go after what is false?" (Ps 4.2-3) And St Gregory the Theologian takes up this Psalmist's interrogation to develop reflections, valid not only for his time but for today also:

> Why do all of you seek so much vanity, seek lie, thinking as it were great the present life, voluptuousness, insignificant glories, worthless posts, and deceitful happiness? Are we not sometimes deciding to turn above to the heaven? Will we not take conscience where we are moving? Will we not stop debauchery of eyes? Will we not learn ever, what is the real wealth, what is the true dignity, and where exists the unbroken power? Which is the unlimited happiness, where to find the unshakeable good, escaping any removal or threat?[119]

St Basil of Caesarea, profound analyst of our interior world, separates the unreal from the real, the instrumental from the false assumption of absolute ownership, a pure fantasy. By proceeding to such an observation, he refutes the illusionary view of his days, as also in our days, that nothing as such is good or evil, but that everything depends on the intention of using or misusing it:

> I come to the conclusion that the one being rich is not subject to jealousy only because of his richness. Neither one in power because of the size of his power, nor the mighty because of the strength of his body, or even a scholar because the abundance of his knowledge.
>
> Because all these mentioned are instruments of virtue provided people use them properly, nothing in themselves and as such possessing blessedness. If one who uses them wrongly is then considered wretched, as the one having received a sword asked to use it for the defense against enemies, he instead willingly tries to kill himself with it.
>
> But if he uses these given things well and reasonably, he then becomes a steward of all that is given by God, becoming rich not for his own exclusive pleasure. It befits rather to be praised and be loved for his attitude for the common good thinking of his brothers and the society.[120]

In such simple reflections the Archbishop of Caesarea offers a right solution to the social conflicts and inequalities, the cause of so many disorders and revolutions since, not raising the poor against the rich, or blaming like the Manicheans, the wealth as such, but by pointing out that we need to change our attitude towards all privileges and gifts, convinced that we are simply mandated administrators and obedient servants.

Many of us are puzzled by the proliferation of atheism and materialism. Nevertheless, atheism is not due to the absence of proofs for God's existence. And the Fathers were aware that the root of the problem does not lie in the incapacity of providing positive arguments for the refutation of error. They avoided such tactics. And instead, they tried to permeate the inner depth of man's world and to show the terrible vacuum and desert without any reference to God.

The ancient and the true Gnostics and Neo-gnostics claim: "Either God wanted the existence of evil, and in such case he is not good; or he did not want it, and therefore is not almighty; in this or that case, he is not God." Such dialectics fail because in life, as in all dealings of God towards humanity, there is a profound mystery, a saving process, and therefore impossible to resolve. Only by faith, deep faith, one can explain the antinomies and strange ways of God's economy in history and in the life of each individual. The Fathers point at the desperate need of God, not only for the sake of the belief in his existence, but for solving all proceeding problems during our existence on earth. Life cannot be explained without reference to God. Thirst, continuous thirst, is a proof of the existence of water!

Many assume that the Fathers belong to the past, only to history. Between the *then* and the *now* there is a break in time and events, so many new problems, and little is to be gained by referring to such bygone, obsolete authors. They lived in a different time, and thus are quite irrelevant. And, yet, as we have seen, while historical events change and humanity witnesses colossal upheavals, both ideological and cultural, man remains in essence the same. It is indeed astonishing how these Fathers made such a deep diagnosis with almost transhistoric eyes, seizing the roots of evils and proposing appropriate remedies. Equally, it is astonishing how the Fathers can say so much which is useful, saving and redeeming for every situation, case or age. They are knowledgeable about almost everything, for almost everybody, most competent in whatever place or age. They have right pronouncements for all areas and fields of this life and the life to come.

How can we explain such extraordinary wisdom? They are of course human, but also more than human, because they are inspired by continuous communion with God's Spirit from where they draw inspiration, supreme knowledge and gifted guidelines. If we listen to them, we might discover how they know everything today, as if they were present and if they were well informed how they see realities and speaking directly just to the point where it concerns us. Their penetrating ability and admonitions on how to get out of impasses and complicated dilemmas is extraordinary. They have thus become our contemporaries. They take up the fundamental questions with a responsible attitude, conscious of their being called to be in the service of man. This is their diaconal contribution, and we recognize it when we reach their teaching through the patristic texts.

There is no period of Church history which did not record errors, distortions of truth, falsifications, heterodoxies, heresies. Facing the irritated congregations, in insecurity and uncertainty, waiting for an authoritative guidance, councils were convoked, synods were summoned, and the Church Fathers were intervening to give the necessary instructions and clarifications. Not only concerning doctrine, but through doctrine to specify existential issues so that Christians might live in accordance with the spirit of the Gospel. The contribution of these Fathers must be seen in such a perspective, their views directly related to vital realities, seeking to improve the quality of religious life, and life in general.

The Church, that is the whole people of God, knows from experience what it owes to these saintly men. Gratitude to them and the consequent feelings are implemented in the liturgical hymnography. In each feast known as the "Feast of the Holy Fathers" we sing the following hymn which covers all aspects of patristics' help for sustaining struggling Christians in their spiritual warfare: "Most glorious are You, O Christ our God, who established our Fathers, as torchbearers on earth and through them guided us all to the true faith, Most Compassionate One, glory to You."[121]

References

[1] *In Origenem oratio panegyrica*, 15; PG 10.1093-6.
Gregory Thaumaturgus, *Address to Origen.* trans. W. Metcalfe. (London, 1920) p. 82.

[2] *Martyrdom of Polycarp* 12.2

[3] Eusebios, *Eccl. Hist.* 5.4,2

[4] Letter 140, 2 and *On the Holy Spirit* 7,16; PG 32.96

[5] *Sacra Parallela;* PG 94-96

[6] PL 59. 597

[7] *To Those Who Rely on the Majority;* PG 28. 1341

[8] *The Ladder*, Step 27, 26

[9] *Philokalia*, Directions from his *Twenty Epistles,* 51

[10] *Homily* 21

[11] *Homily* 71

[12] *The Orthodox Faith.* 90

[13] *Contra Graec.* 1; PG 25.4

[14] B. Laourdas, *Photios' Homilies* (Thessalonike, 1959), p. 155
[15] *Sermon* 21, 1 PG 35.844
[16] *Oratio* 21 *in laudem Athanasii,* 5; pg 35. 1088
[17] Ep 107 *ad Laetam*; PL 22. 877
[18] *Life of Anthony* 48, 56-37, 81
[19] Ibid. 88
[20] St. Makarios, *Epistula ad filios* 1; also 11
[21] *Life of Anthony* 23
[22] *Verba Seniorum* 7, 15, 2; PL 73, 1038
[23] *Apostolic Constitutions* 2,26, 4
[24] Ibid. 2, 20, 1-2, and 2, 33, 1
[25] *Apophtegmata Patrum*: Anthony, 18
[26] *Centuries*, 1,28
[27] *Hymns* 15
[28] *Sayings of the Desert Fathers:* Longinus
[29] *Ascetic Instructions*
[30] *Encomion to St Basil*; PG 36, 560
[31] Athanasios, *Letter to Adelphion*; PG 26.1077
[32] *De incarnatione* 53; PG 25, 126
[33] *Sermon on Symeon and Anna*; PG 18.361
[34] *The Orthodox Faith* PG 94.1032
[35] *Ad Thalassius;* PG 90.412A; see also *Theol. Centuries* 2; PG 90.1172D
[36] *City*
[37] Letter 2 to Gregory
[38] *Theological Sermons* 5
[39] *Letter to Sosandrus;* PG 79.169
[40] PG 82. 879-1280
[41] PG 82.1284-1521
[42] PG 82.1497
[43] William Johnston, *Post-Modernisme et Bimillenaire: Le culte des anniversaires dans la culture contemporaire* (Paris, 1992).
[44] *Life of Anthony* 3.4; PG 26.844-45
[45] Ibid. 46
[46] *Homilia in illud, attende tibi ipsi,* 2; PG 31.201
[47] *Sermon* 6th, *Eirenic*
[48] *Supplication for the Christians*
[49] *On the Freedom of Will*
[50] *Comment in Song of Songs;* PG 649 BC
[51] *On the inscript. of Ps*; PG 44.557B
[52] Consecratory Prayer, Divine Liturgy of St John Chrysostom
[53] *Apologeticum* 46

[54] *Apophtegmata*, Longin 5; PG 65.275; See Dorotheos of Gaza, *Instructions* 10, 104
[55] *Laws* B,6 59D
[56] Verses 16-19
[57] *Phaedo* 28, E
[58] *Anacharsis* 15,893
[59] *Sermon* 4, 28; *Steliteuticos* 1; PG 35.636
[60] PG 31.563-90
[61] *Apologeticus* 50
[62] *Hom.* 75. 4-5 on St. John; PG 59.409
[63] *Sermon* 4,6 *on Beatitudes*
[64] *Fifth Theol. Centuries,* 99
[65] Fragments 26; PG 7.1244
[66] *Comment. on Ps* 109.9; PG 55.279
[67] *Comment. on Ps* 109. 9; PG 55.279
[68] Diog. Laert. *Lives* 6, 3; Loeb ed. 185, 4
[69] Idem 6, 8; Loeb 185, 20
[70] Idem 185, 72
[71] Menex. 246E
[72] *Homily* 19,5 *on Hebrews*
[73] *The Ladder,* Step 25
[74] *Gerontikon* 74
[75] *The Ladder,* Step 15,2
[76] *Homily* 46
[77] *Homily* 2 *on the 37 Psalm*; PG 12.1386
[78] *Sermon I to the Fathers;* PG 99.688
[79] *City* 4, 424 A
[80] *Comment. on 37 Psalm*; PG 12.1386
[81] *Sermon 2 Apologetic* 71; PG 35.480B
[82] *Traicte de l'employ des Saincts Peres pour le jugement des differends qui sont sujourd'hui en la Religion.* (Geneva, 1632) p. 529.
[83] *Adversus Haereses,* 4, 26, 1; 11,234
[84] PG 10.1093A
[85] *Homil. on Genesis* 7,6
[86] *De Ecclesiastica Hierarchia* 3, 7; PG 3.513
[87] *Sermon* 63, 7; PL 54.3S7C
[88] *De Divinis Nominibus* 2,2; PG 3.674
[89] *Epist.* 118.32; PL 33.448
[90] *Contra Arianos* 2.3; PG 26.152
[91] *Against Eunomius* 2.4; PG 29.580
[92] *De Principiis,* praef. 3 and 10
[93] *Contra Celsum,* 3, 52
[94] *Opus imp. contra Jul.* 1, 117; PL 45. 125

[95] *Dialogue against Heresies*, 365; PG 155.33-696
[96] *Dialogue* Ch. 365
[97] Sophie Antoniades, *Place de la Liturgie dans la tradition des Lettres Greques* (Leiden, 1939)
[98] Translation B; Botte; SC 11, 1946
[99] Chapters nine and ten
[100] Martin Luther, *Deutsche Messe*, 1526.
[101] *La forme des prieres et des chantz ecclesistiques avec la maniere d'administrer les sacraments et consacrer le mariage selon la coutume de l'Eglise ancienne*, (Geneva, 1542).
[102] Andre Benoit, *L'actualite des Peres de l'Eglise* (Neuchatel, 1961), p. 75-6.
[103] PG 35.785
[104] PG 46.244
[105] Anatolius of Studium, Second *Sticheron*
[106] Third *Sticheron*
[107] *Sticheron* of Vespers
[108] Palladius: *Laus. Hist.* 10; PG 34.1148AB; Rufinus: *Hist. Mon.* 7; PL 21.418BC
[109] *Oratio Panegyrica* 14-15; PG 10.1093
[110] *In Origenem panegyrica*, 15; PG 10.1093-96.
[111] *Ch. Hist.* 6,45
[112] *Epistola* 2, PG 10.1296
[113] *Epistola* 3; PG 10.1296-1312
[114] PG 10.1313-6 and Eusebius: *Church Hist.* 7, 5
[115] *Contra Celsum* 1, 52
[116] *Hom.* 11 *in Hebrews*; PG 62.87
[117] PG 47.701
[118] *Sermon on martyr Phocas* 2; PG 50.700
[119] *Sermon* 19.4: PG 35.1048
[120] *Sermon* 11.5 *on Envy*; PG 31.384
[121] *Troparion* of the 1st Ecumen. Council, Tone 8

Index

Adam 32
Adonai 76
AIDS 51, 52
Aischylos 35
Akakios, Abba 14
Alexandria 51, 64, 65, 66
Alexandrian (Fathers) 6
Andrew of Crete 42
Antiochian (Fathers) 6
Antisthenes 44
Apeles 63
Apollonius 65
Apollos 77
Apostles 5, 57
Areopagos 37
Arianism 10, 58
Arians 9
Aristotle 19, 79
Arius 62
Asia 2, 63
Assyrians 22
Athenagoras the Apologist 30, 65
Athenasios of Alexandria, St 9, 11, 20, 62, 79
Athenians 37
Athens 65
Augustine, St 18, 20, 59, 67
Augustus 76
Aurelius, Marcus 30, 63

Babylon 64
Barth, Karl 81
Basil of Caesarea, St 2, 5, 22, 28, 30, 37, 62, 71, 74, 91, 92
Basilides 63
Bible 2, 4, 5, 9, 10, 53, 70, 71, 72, 74
Byzantine (Fathers) 6

Calvin, John 53, 72
Cappadocian (Fathers) 6
Cassia 76
Celsus 66
Charismatic Movement 4
Cherubim 75
Christ (Jesus) 5, 8, 9, 11, 15, 18, 19, 37, 41, 47, 54, 56, 57, 58, 59, 65, 68, 72, 73, 75, 77, 798
Christian(s) 18, 26, 30, 40, 41, 44, 45, 46, 47, 53, 54, 56, 64, 65, 74, 77, 84, 88
Christianity 37, 50; Latin 4
Chrysippos 63
Chrysostom, John St 39, 41, 42, 45, 51, 71, 86, 87
Chrysostom, Pseudo 71
Church *passim*
Clement of Alexandria 27, 64, 65
Commodus 30, 66
Constantine the Great 38
Constantinople 10, 15, 75
Council Ecumenical, 69, 70, 76; Nicaea 9, 76; Ephesos 58

Decius 85
Devil 47
Diogenes 44
Dion of Prusa 63
Dionysios of Alexandria 85
Dionysios the Areopagite, St 58, 59, 85
Dionysios, Pseudo 71

Egypt 15
Egyptians 22
Ekklesia 8
Eleutherios (Pope) 2
Elijah 60
Elisha 60
Eloha 76
Elohim 76
Emmaus 5
Epicureans 37
Epiktetos 44, 64

Epikuros 63
Eucharist 32
Eunomios 62
Europe 29
Eusebios 11

Fabius of Antioch 85
Fathers, Church *passim*; Nicaean 58
Felix, Abba 13

Galilee 51
Genesis, Book of 32
Geneva 55, 72
Germanos of Constantionople 75
Gnostics 64, 72, 92
God *passim*
Gospel 4, 5, 81, 82, 87
Greeks 44, 76
Gregory of Nyssa, St 31, 39, 75
Gregory the Theologian (Nazianzos), St 10, 18, 22, 30, 36, 50, 59, 71, 73, 74, 80, 91
Gregory the Wonder-worker 1, 57

Hellenism 37
Heracleon 63, 66
Heterokles 35
Hierotheos 59
Hippolytus 64, 71
Horeb 75

Ignatios of Antioch, St 64
Irenaios, St 57, 64
Isaak the Syrian, St 7, 18
Isidore 63
Israel 15, 55, 56, 70

James, St 71, 74
Japan 29
Jehova 75
Jeremiah 8
Jerome, St 11
Jews 51, 76
John Damascene, St 2, 8, 18
John Klimakos, St 6, 46, 47
John the Baptist, St 56
John, St (the Evangelist) 49, 66
Jordan River 60
Joshua 59
Julian the Apostate 36, 37
Justin 64, 65

Kleopas 5

Leo the Great, St 59
Leontios of Cyprus 32
Liturgy, Divine 69
Logos 30, 36, 44, 63, 65
Longinos 14
Lucian 36
Luther, Martin 53
Lycia 30

Makarios, Pseudo 71
Makarios, St 12
Marcionites 72
Mathoes, Abba 47
Maxim of Tyra 63
Maximos the Confessor, St 18, 40
Methodios of Olympos 18, 30
Middle East 62
Moses 15, 22, 23, 60, 75
Moshe 76
Musonios 63

Nestorios 58
New Testament 9, 26, 56, 69, 82
Nicaea 58
Nilos the Ascetic 23
Novatian 85
Nun 60

Old Testament 48, 55, 56, 63, 69, 70, 72, 73
Olympic Games 36
Origen 1, 27, 48, 50, 57, 63, 64, 66, 73, 80, 81, 86
Orthodox 53, 59

Palestine 79
Palladius 11
Pambo, Abbot 47
Pantainos 27
Paphos 20
Paul St 11, 37, 50, 64
Perennis 65
Pergamun 65
Photios, St 10
Pistias 61
Plato 35, 44, 79
Plutarch 63, 66
Polycarp of Smyrna, St 2
Presancitified Gifts 71
Protestants 55
Proverbs, Book of 39
Ptolemy the Gnostic 63

Reformers 53
Roman Catholics 55
Roman Empire 18, 38
Rome 2
Rufinus 11

Saccas, Ammonius 63
Scriptures 5, 37, 54, 55, 57, 63, 64, 70; Hebrew 56
Secundus 63
Socrates 11, 61
Solon 36
Son of God 63
Sozomen 11
Spirit (Holy) 4, 10, 11, 14, 25, 48, 49, 67, 69, 73
Stephen of Rome 85
Stoics 37
Studios Monastery 14
Symeon of Thessalonike, St 70
Symeon the New Theologian, St 14, 19
Symeon the Pious 14
Syncretism 37
Syria 60, 63
Syriac 6

Tatian 64, 65
Tertullian 33, 38
Thebes 35
Theodore Studite, St 49
Theodoret of Kyros 23
Trinity, Holy 48

Valentinus 30, 63, 66
Virgin 75

Yahweh 22

Made in the USA
Coppell, TX
15 June 2024

33536066R00069